Larry A. Maxwell

What Does the Bible Say About Animals And Where Do Animals Go When They Die?

An In-depth Look

By

Dr. Larry A. Maxwell

Larry A. Maxwell

This Book is Dedicated to Three People
Who Exemplify Proverbs 12:10

John Simpson
My Friend, a First Responder, a Nurse
A Rescuer and Faithful Friend to Katrina and Beekman

Peter Maycott
My Friend, a First Responder, Loving Husband to Edith
A Friend, Provider and Protector of Dogs

Grace Maxwell
My Daughter, a Teacher, a Librarian
A Rescuer, Protector and Friend of Cats

Cover Image: *Adam Naming the Creatures* by Currier & Ives

All scripture used in this book are from the
Authorized King James Version of the Bible.

Publisher

Challenge International
1130 Perry Rd., Afton, NY 13730
599 Route 311, Patterson, Ny 12563

ISBN: 978-1-949277-13-5

Table of Contents

Chapter	Page

Larry A. Maxwell

Editorial Note

There are times in this book when I refer to humans as *man*. That use of the word *man*, is the biblical and scientific usage of that word, which means *mankind*. It does not refer exclusively to men but to both men and woman. The term mankind is ironic because too often many men are not kind.

List of Illustrations

Many of the illustrations in this book are from old Bibles or old theological books.

A number of the illustrations are by the French artist Paul Louise Christophe Gustave Dore. He is often referred to as Gustave Dore. Dore was born in Strasbourg, France in 1832 and died in Paris in 1883. He was known especially for his wood and steel engravings. He was a self-taught artist. He produced more than 100,000 sketches in his lifetime.

Some of the illustrations are from the book <u>Bible Animals</u> by Rev. J. G. Wood, published in 1883 in London, by Longmans, Green and Co. The illustrations in that book are by W.F. Keyl, T.W. Wood and A. E. Smith. The book does not attribute the specific artist for each illustration.

Introduction

The original purpose of this book was to answer to the question, *where do animals go when they die?* As this book was being written, that changed. Answering that question is still the focus of this book but answering that question required addressing some other important issues related to animals.

Animals are very dear to many people. When an animal is facing death, or has died, that is often a difficult time. Many want to comfort those who are hurting and try to say something kind. They mean well but in that difficult time it is important to understand the answer to the question, *where do animals go when they die?* Knowing the answer to that question can help provide lasting comfort.

To be truly helpful and comforting, the answer to that question needs to be more than just someone's personal opinion. It needs to come from an authoritative source which deals with questions of life and death, and of what follows. There is only one source which claims that authority. That source if the Bible, the Word of God.

One of the harsh realities of life is one day, every animal and person will die. Some will live longer than others but one day death comes to every living creature.

When we face the possibility of our own death, or the death of a loved one, many consider the question, *where will I, or my loved ones, go when we die?* Those who care for animals often ask the same question.

Over the years I discovered children, who in many cases are usually the ones farthest removed from death, seem to be the ones most sensitive to it. When a pet becomes ill, or dies, some children ask, *Where will my pet go when they die?* Many ask, *Will I see my pet again?* Some ask, *Will my pet go to Heaven?*

If you lost a pet, and ask those questions, some may try

to comfort you and tell you your pet went to Heaven, even if they are not convinced of that. People hold different views on this and will give different answers. Some will bluntly tell you when an animal dies it ceases to exist.

Which answer is correct? When it comes to important questions like, *where do animals go when they die*, we need more than someone's personal opinion.

In this book I try to do more than just give my opinion. My opinion by itself may not be worth very much to someone else. In this book I set out to try to show you how I arrived at my opinion. I believe the Bible is God's revealed word to us. I came to the conclusions in this book after years of experience and carefully studying the Bible.

To help answer the question, *where do animals go when they die*, I believe it is helpful to take an in-depth look at exactly what the Bible says about animals. In this book we will look at where animals came from and why they were made. We will see how they are similar to mankind yet different.

Some of the things the Bible says about animals may surprise you. For example, did you know there are some talking animals in the Bible? Did you know there are some animal-like extra-terrestrial beings in the Bible?

In this book you will see how the God of the Bible is described with some animal-like characteristics.

I love animals. I always have. I grew up in a household which had a variety of pets. At different times in my life we had dogs, cats, birds, fish, and a turtle. My mother's father even had a monkey.

Like me, many people have strong emotional connections with some animals. That love and concern is very real and meaningful. That love can go both ways. Animals can be closer to some people than family or friends.

One of my parishioners, Sandra Seymour, loves animals. She calls them *anipals*. I discovered she did not create that term. The *Online Urban Dictionary* has a listing for *anipal*. It defines an anipal as *a pet that is also a close friend*.

One of my favorite actors, John Wayne, shared that same sentiment. I will never forget in one movie he said something like this, *Horses and dogs are man's best friends. They never ask for anything except to be loved.* That expresses my sentiments quite well.

Many people know God loves mankind. The Bible tells us that.

For God so loved the world, He gave His only begotten Son, that whosoever believeth in Him should not perish but have everlasting life   John 3:16

The Bible also tells us God wants each one of us to live forever with Him in a wonderful place called Heaven.

Let not your heart be troubled, believe in God, believe also in me. In my Father's house are many mansions. If t were not so, I would have told you. I go to prepare a place for you, that where I am there you may be also.
                                        John 14:1-3

It is estimated there are almost 8 billion people in the world. Each one of those 8 billion people is important to God. The Bible says God knows each of them by name.

Because He (God) hath set His love upon me, therefore I will deliver him: I will set Him on high, because He hath known my name.   Psalm 91:14

It is important to understand, not only does God care about every human, but He also cares for every animal.

Are not two sparrows sold for farthing? And not one of them shall fall on the ground without your father.
                                        Matthew 10:29

Sparrows are the most common bird in the world. They are often considered a bird of little value. The Bible tells us God knows when even one sparrow dies.

The world's population of birds is estimated between 200 to 400 billion. There are billions more of them than there are of humans, yet God knows about the fate of each one of them.

In this book we will see how much God cares for animals. That fact and other interesting truths all work together and help answer the question, *where do animals go when they die?*

Hopefully, you will find some interesting, helpful, and comforting information in this book.

Chapter 1

Where Did Animals Come From?

To answer the question, *where do animals go when they die?* first, we need to answer the question, *where did animals come from?*

A person's view as to the origin of animals, greatly effects their view as to where animals go when they die.

There are three basic schools of thought as to where animals came from. One view teaches animals, as well as everything else on earth, came into being by chance. According to that view animals exist as a result of a process called *Natural Selection*.

Natural Selection is part of the *theory of evolution*. It teaches all life forms evolved by chance, over millions of years. According to that theory, stronger life forms triumphed over weaker ones, until the weaker ones passed out of existence. That theory teaches there is no designer, no predetermination of function, and no intrinsic value for anything or anyone. According to that theory every life is here as a result of the *survival of the fittest*.

Another school of thought regarding the origin of animals, which gained more followers in recent years, teaches animals and life on earth came here from somewhere else. Some believe life arrived here randomly, perhaps on a meteor. Some teach life was placed here by superior extraterrestrial beings from some other galaxy or dimension. Some believe those extraterrestrials placed us here and left us alone. Some believe they are keeping an eye on us.

The third school of thought regarding the origin of animals, which I follow, and which ironically has been thrown out of most schools, teaches animals and all life on earth was created by an intelligent Creator called God. I believe that intelligent Creator is the God of the Bible. In one sense the God of the Bible is extraterrestrial, in the sense He is not from this world. He is also so much more. He is not only not from our world, but also the one who created our world and everything in the universe.

EDEN, IN THE MORNING OF CREATION.

Eden in the Morning of Creation
*The Beautiful Story: A Companion Book to the Holy Bible,
J.W. Buel, Boston MA: Eastern Publishing Co., 1888*

You may wonder, why does a person's view on where animals came from make a difference? Consider this, if you believe animals came into being by Natural Selection, that means you believe they do not have any pre-designed intrinsic value or meaning. That means it is only natural for the weaker ones to die off and pass into oblivion. That view has a simple answer to the question, *where do animals go when they die?* According to that view, when animals die, they cease to exist and go back to nothing.

If you believe extraterrestrial beings made the animals, then you believe they were designed and made with a specific purpose. That purpose, along with what happens when animals die, can be hard to determine without further information.

On the other hand, if you believe animals were made by God, you can look to God to find the answer to the question, *where do animals go when they die?*

The Bible claims it is the word of God. Unlike other books it is not a compilation of writings or stories about God. It claims to be absolute truth and God's very word.

> *In the beginning was the Word, and the Word was with God, and the Word was God. The same was in the beginning with God. All things were made by him; and without him was not any thing made that was made.*
> John 1:1-3

The Bible specifically says God created this world and all life on it. It addresses our origins. It also gives practical guidance for daily living and reveals some elements of the future and the end of this world as we know it.

The Bible teaches God created all the animals. That means every variety of animal came from God. That means they were designed by Him. None came into existence by chance nor as a result of a struggle with another weaker form of life. Each has a unique purpose. They are important to God. They are so important to God, He gave man the responsibility to take care of them.

Some good people differ on the Biblical teaching, regarding the origin of life and of animals.

Evolution, and its teaching of Natural Selection, conflict with the Biblical teaching of a Creator. They also conflict with good science. They teach life came from a chance combination of certain chemicals and that there is a continual changing among species to evolve and become more advanced.

True science shows life and animals did not arrive here by chance. Look at the following scientific principles, which contradict evolution:

1. **The First Law of Thermodynamics** – This scientific law states matter, and energy, cannot be created or destroyed. That is totally at odds with evolution which teaches things are being created all the time. This law fits perfectly with the Biblical concept of a Creator God who created an expansive universe and all life on earth in six twenty-four-hour days and then stopped creating.

2. **The Second Law of Thermodynamics – The Law of Entropy** – This scientific law teaches things are always breaking down, moving from order to disorder. Things do not evolve and become better. A car turns into rust, rust does not turn into a car. We have more disorder in our world than order because of entropy. Our world is wearing out. That is exactly what the Bible teaches.

3. **The Law of Cause and Effect** –This scientific law teaches for every *effect* there is a *cause*. The cause must be ultimately greater than the effect. That is exactly what the Bible teaches. An infinite God is the cause who created a finite universe.

4. **The Theory of Relativity** – This scientific principle teaches all things in the universe are tied together in a space time continuum. It requires a *beginning* and a *Beginner*. Many evolutionists say the origin of life on our world started as a result of a *big bang*. The problem with that theory is in order for something to explode and make a *big bang*, something had to exist before the *big bang*. They believe there was nothing before that. I believe God

was there at the beginning and is the personal intelligent One who gave a beginning to everything we know.

The Bible teaches a personal loving God, created this world, as well as all animals and mankind. That teaching does not contradict with good science.

In the New Testament, in the Book of First Timothy, there is a warning about people who manipulate science to lead people astray.

> *O Timothy, keep that which is committed to thy trust, avoiding profane and vain babblings, and oppositions of science falsely so called: which some professing have erred from the faith.*   1 Timothy 6:20-21

Neither we, nor animals, are here as a result of a random process. God made all things purposefully and with value. That loving God created man and animals. God then gave man the responsibility to take care of the world and all the animals He created.

Questions for Thought or Discussion
Chapter 1
Where Did Animals Come From?

1. How does a person's view on the origin of animals affect their answer to the question, *where do animals go when they die?*

2. What are the three basic schools of thought regarding the origin of animals?

3. Which view does not place intrinsic value on all animals?

4. What book tells us God created man and animals?

5. How do some scientific principles specifically contradict the theory of evolution?

Chapter 2

Animals Are Similar But Different Than Man

Some people refer to humans as a type of animal. I believe that can be insulting to animals. Some animals behave better than many humans. Perhaps, if humans were animals, they might act better.

The idea man is an animal comes from the theory of evolution. Evolution teaches every living being descended from a common ancestor. It teaches because of accidents, mutations and struggles, different species evolved over millions of years. Weaker species became extinct as they were replaced by stronger better evolved ones. That is called *survival of the fittest*. That directly affects attitudes towards animals as it teaches extinction of certain species is a good and natural part of the process.

Though some teach evolution as a fact, it is only a theory, and it has many weaknesses. Evolution teaches all life forms evolved from simper forms over millions of years. That would mean there should be billions of transitional life forms in the fossil record. Such evidence does not exist except in evolutionary textbooks.

Another weakness of evolution is its teaching that man evolved from apes and became one of the highest forms of evolved life. If man is a higher form of life than apes, why are there still apes and why do some apes act better than some humans?

For years evolutionists used charts showing how man transitioned from apes. The chart include supposed transitional lower life forms such as Neanderthal or Cro-Magnon Man. Both of those have been recognized variations of Homo Sapiens, the classification which includes all variants of modern man.

THE MODERN THEORY OF THE DESCENT OF MAN.

THE ANCESTRY OF MAN, *traced by naturalist Ernst Haeckel in 1867, was one of the first attempts to deal with the specifics of evolution. Although his genealogical chart, starting* *with a blob of protoplasm and continuing to a modern Papuan, is filled with misconceptions and fictitious creatures, it is fairly accurate, considering the dearth of knowledge in his day.*

The Modern Theory of the Descent of Man
By Ernst Heinrich Philippi August Haeckel, 1867

Jean-Baptiste Lamarck (1744-1829) is considered one of the founders of evolutionary teaching. He taught the environment caused changes in animals over time, causing newer and more complex organisms. Lamarck's colleague,

Étienne Geoffroy Saint-Hilaire (1772-1844), expanded on Lamarck's teaching and said species could transmute into other species. Their teaching were popularized by Charles Darwin who expanded their teachings to include a link between animals and humans.

Darwin never had any formal scientific training. He attended the University of Cambridge in England, with the intention of becoming a clergyman. The only degree he earned was a basic Bachelor of Arts degree, the prerequisite degree for ministerial studies.

Darwin wrote a book in which he set forth his teachings of Evolution and Natural Selection. Most educators only use part of the title of Darwin's book. The title is usually listed as, *The Origin of Species*. The full title is, *The Origin of Species by Means of Natural Selection, Or the Preservation of the Favoured Races in the Struggle of Life.*

Darwin also expanded on pervious teachings which attempted to classify humans by their physical appearance.

In 1684, Francois Bernier classified people as belonging to one of four geographic groups: Europeans, Far Easterners, Blacks, and Lapps.

In 1775, Johann Friedrich Blumenbach, published a scientific treatise classifying humans as belonging to four different geographic classifications. In 1795, Blumenbach expanded that to include five different classifications. They were called: Americans, Caucasians, Ethiopians, Malays, and Mongolians.

In his writings, though Blumenbach identified some differences between his five categories, he emphasized there were no clear cut subdivision of human species. There was only one Human race.

Darwin's took those classifications a step further and used his theory of evolution to explain the differences. He taught lighter skinned people, like he, were more evolved than darker colored people. According to him, the darker races, such as the Africans and Native Australians were closer to apes than humans and were not fully evolved.

Darwin expanded his offensive and racist premise in his

book, *The Descent of Man,* as well as in other writings.

In 1863, Darwin published a paper called, *On the Negroes Place in Nature*. In that paper, he taught slavery was beneficial to what he called *the less evolved races.*

His teachings were embraced by racists worldwide. They were used to justify slavery and mistreatment of what others saw as, *inferior races.*

Darwin's teaching were opposed by conservative Christians who taught all were created equal.

Classifying people as belonging to different races fosters prejudice. Though there are some physical differences between some groups of people, there is still only one race. It is the Human Race.

It is amazing Darwin's racist books and teachings are allowed to be used in any educational institution.

Darwin's claim, placing man at the height of the evolutionary chain, reinforces the devaluation of animals. For Darwin, and his fellow evolutionists, different species are only stepping stones to producing better, more evolved species. That causes people to view some species as inferior.

Evolutionists teach the similarities between man and ape are because of evolution. They ignore the fact man and apes are different species and both existed simultaneously since they were created.

Evolutionists believe the fact dogs, cats, and many animals, have common characteristics means they share a common ancestor. The real reason man and animals have similarities is because we share a common loving Creator. That Creator purposefully made man and every different species of animal.

All humans and all animals are beautiful and valuable in God's eyes and should be valuable in our eyes.

Some of the similarities between man and animals, play a role in answering the question, *where do animals go when they die?*

> *And the very God of peace sanctify you wholly; and I pray God your whole spirit and soul and body be*

preserved blameless unto the coming of our Lord Jesus
Christic. 1 Thessalonians 5:23

The Bible teaches man is made of three parts, a *body*, a *soul*, and a *spirit*.

The body responds to our environment with its five senses: sight, smell, hearing, touch, and taste. It is obvious we all have a body. If you do not have a body, you are nobody.

God created man and each species of animals with distinct bodies. All humans and animals have bodies. If you are sitting in a room and hear a barking sound, there is probably a dog nearby. If the barking sound gets louder, and you do not see a dog, there is a problem. If the barking continues and you feel something jump in your lap and still do not see a dog that should concern you. Dogs have bodies.

All flesh is not the same flesh: but there is one kind of
flesh of men, another flesh of beasts, another of fishes,
and another of birds. 1 Corinthians 15:39

Cowboys and Horses from Word of Life
In a July 4th Parade in Schroon Lake, N.Y.
It is obvious they have distinctly different bodies.
Photograph by Larry A. Maxwell

Evolutionists teach man evolved from animals. Some say the fact the Bible says man was made after animals reinforces their theory. The Biblical description of how animals and man were made contradicts that.

And God said, Let the earth bring forth the living creature after his kind, cattle, and creeping thing, and beast of the earth after his kind: and it was so.
Genesis 1:24

God created animals by speaking words. He made humans in a different way. Unlike animals, God *formed man* from the dust of the ground. It should humble us to know, He made us from dirt.

And the LORD God formed man of the dust of the ground, and breathed into his nostrils the breath of life; and man became a living soul. Genesis 2:7

The Bible also teaches man was made in *the image of God*. The Hebrew word in the Bible for *image* means *something which looks similar*.

So God created man in his own image, in the image of God created he him; male and female created he them.
Genesis 1:27

Though both man and animals have bodies, and though they have some similarities, it appears man's bodies look more like God.

In numerous instances in the Bible, when God appeared to man He appeared in what appeared to be a human form.

And the LORD appeared unto him (Abraham) in the plains of Mamre: and he sat in the tent door in the heat of the day; And he lift up his eyes and looked, and, lo, three men stood by him: and when he saw them, he ran to meet them from the tent door, and bowed himself toward the ground. Genesis 18:1-2

Not only do men have a *body*, but we also have a *soul*. The soul interacts with those around us. It is comprised of three parts: the *mind*, the *emotions* and the *will*.

Everyone has a *mind*, though there are times some people may seem like they lost theirs. We all have *emotions*, though some are more emotional than others. And we all have a *will*, the part of our soul which makes choices.

In the Hebrew Scriptures, the word for *soul* is *nephesh*. That word is used in the Book of Genesis 2:7, where it makes it clear man has a soul.

> *The Lord God formed man of the dust of the ground, and breathed into his nostrils the breath of life and man became a living soul (nephesh).*　　　　Genesis 2:7

In Deuteronomy 4:9, it says we should be sure to keep our souls and not let our hearts depart from Him.

> *Only take heed to thyself, and keep thy soul (nephesh) diligently, lest thou forget the things which thine eyes have seen, and lest they depart from thy heart all the days of thy life: but teach them thy sons, and thy sons' sons.*　　　　Deuteronomy 4:9

In Deuteronomy 6:5, it says we are to love God with all our heart, all our soul, and all our might (bodies).

> *And thou shalt love the LORD thy God with all thine heart, and with all thy soul, and with all thy might.*
> 　　　　Deuteronomy 6:5

Both Psalm 16:10 and Psalm 86:13, refer to delivering a soul from an afterlife in an awful place called Hell.

> *For thou wilt not leave my soul in hell; neither wilt thou suffer thine Holy One to see corruption.*
> 　　　　Psalm 16:10

> *For great is thy mercy toward me: and thou hast delivered my soul from the lowest hell.*　　Psalm 86:13

Though most agree all humans have a soul, many do not believe animals have souls. Yet, the Bible clearly says animals have souls. Genesis 1:20-21 describes part of the account of the fifth day of the creation.

> *And God said, Let the waters bring forth abundantly the moving creature that hath life (nephesh) , and fowl that*

may fly above the earth in the open firmament of heaven. And God created great whales, and every living creature (nephesh) that moveth, which the waters brought forth abundantly, after their kind, and every winged fowl after his kind: and God saw that it was good. Genesis 1:20-21

The Hebrew word, *nephesh* (soul) is translated in these verses as *life,* and as *living creature.* These verses make it clear creatures which live in the water, as well as winged fowl, all have souls. That is not talking about men.

And God said, Let the earth bring forth the living creature (nephesh) after his kind (species), cattle and creeping thing, and beast of the earth after his kind, and it was so. Genesis 1:24

Genesis 1:24 makes it clear cattle, and all other creatures which live on the land, have souls.

In Genesis 9:10, where the Bible tells the account of Noah taking the animals on an ark, before the flood, it refers to both the birds and animals as having souls.

And with every living creature (nephesh) that is with you, of the fowl, of the cattle, and of every beast of the earth with you; from all that go out of the ark, to every beast of the earth. Genesis 9:10

Now look at the New Testament. Most of the New Testament was written in Greek. The Greek word used in the New Testament for soul is *psuche.*

In 1 Thessalonians 5:23, it says man is comprised of a spirt, a soul (*psuche*) and a body.

And the very God of peace sanctify you wholly; and I pray God your whole spirit and soul (psuche) and body be preserved blameless unto the coming of our Lord Jesus Christ. I Thessalonians 5:23

In the *Gospel of Matthew*, it says the body and soul (*psuche*) can end up in the afterlife in a place called Hell. Thankfully, other verses tell us how to avoid that.

And fear not them which kill the body, but are not able

> *to kill the soul: but rather fear him which is able to*
> *destroy both soul and body in hell.*   Matthew 10:28

In the *Book of Revelation*, it speaks of every living soul (*psuche*) dying *in* the ocean. Humans do not live *in* the ocean. That reinforces Genesis 1:25, letting us know all sea creatures have souls.

> *And the second angel poured out his vial upon the sea;*
> *and it became as the blood of a dead man: and every*
> *living soul died in the sea.*   Revelation 16:3

The Bible clearly teaches animals have bodies and souls. The fact animals have souls, raises another question. Can animals have some of the same soul problems as man? I believe they can and do. That is a topic for another book.

Man also has a third part, that third part is called the spirit. We have seen, like man, animals have bodes and souls but do animals have spirits?

The *spirit* is associated with the *soul*, but different. Both the Hebrew Scriptures and the New Testament teach us it can be hard to distinguish between the two.

> *With my soul have I desired thee in the night; yea, with*
> *my spirit within me will I seek thee early: for when thy*
> *judgments are in the earth, the inhabitants of the world*
> *will learn righteousness.*   Isaiah 26:9

> *For the word of God is quick, and powerful, and sharper*
> *than any twoedged sword, piercing even to the dividing*
> *asunder of soul and spirit, and of the joints and marrow,*
> *and is a discerner of the thoughts and intents of the*
> *heart.*   Hebrews 4:12

The word in the Hebrew Scriptures for *spirit* is *ruwach*. That word is used for the Spirit of God (Genesis 1:2). It is also used for the spirit of man (Job 32;8; Job 33:4; Psalm 31:5; Psalm 32:2).

In Genesis, God let Noah know the world would soon be destroyed by a worldwide flood.

> *And, behold, I, even I, do bring a flood of water upon the*
> *earth, to destroy all flesh, wherin is the breath of life*

(ruwach), from under heaven, and everything that is in the earth shall die. Genesis 6:17

This verse refers to *all flesh*, every living thing, as having a *spirit*. That means animals have a spirit.

The Greek word in the New Testament for *spirit* is *pneuma*. In some passages it refers to the Holy Spirit.

And Jesus, when he was baptized, went up straightway out of the water: and, lo, the heavens were opened unto him, and he saw the Spirit of God descending like a dove, and lighting upon him. Matthew 3:16

In other passages, it refers to man's spirit.

For what man knoweth the things of a man, save the spirit of man which is in him? even so the things of God knoweth no man, but the Spirit of God. 1 Corinthians 2:11

It is interesting to note the Bible refers to man as being spiritually dead (Ephesians 2:1-8). The Bible never says that about animals. Spiritual death, and the part animals played in providing a solution for man, will be addressed in the next chapter.

And you hath he quickened, who were dead in trespasses and sin. Ephesians 2:1

In this chapter we saw man and animals are different, yet similar. Each have a body, a soul, and a spirit. That is a significant truth when we consider the question, *where do animals go when they die?*

Questions for Thought or Discussion
Chapter 2
Animals are Similar
But Different Than Man

1. Where did the idea come from that man is an animal?

2. How does the teaching of the theory of evolution and survival of the fittest effect people's views of animals?

3. What is especially offensive about the teachings of Charles Darwin and what evil practice did it condone?

4. What is the difference between how God created animals and man?

5. What are the three parts which make up a man?

6. What three parts make up the soul? Do animals have souls?

7. What is the spirit? Do animals have spirits?

Chapter 3

The Sin Problem

Every human sins. As a result, the world is filled with sin and the awful consequences of that sin. Many never consider the effect their sin has on others, much less the effect it has on animals.

For all have sinned, and come short of the glory of God.
Romans 3:23

What is sin? Sin is anything contrary to God's perfect plan for our lives. Sin includes *attitudes* and our *actions*.

God has a special plan for each of our lives. It involves a great relationship with Him and with others. His plan for us will bring us fulfillment and great joy if we accept it. The problem is too often we choose to sin instead of doing what God wants us to do.

Sin has extremely negative effects. It hurts us and often those around us, including animals. Sin separates us from God and from each other. It stops us from experiencing the wonderful fulfilling life God designed for us.

God hates sin and wants us to hate it. If we hated sin, we would not sin, and the world would be a better place.

Death is one of the most serious consequences of sin. God told Adam and Eve, the first man and woman, if they sinned, they would die.

Back in the Garden of Eden, Adam and Eve had unlimited freedom. God gave them only one restriction.

And the LORD God commanded the man, saying, Of every tree of the garden thou mayest freely eat: But of the tree of the knowledge of good and evil, thou shalt not eat of it: for in the day that thou eatest thereof thou shalt surely die. Genesis 2:16-17

God said if they ate from that one tree, the day they did that, they would die. What did God mean by that?

Many know Adam and Eve ate from that tree. How did that happen, and what was the result of their actions?

It is important to understand though Adam and Eve were the only humans in the Garden of Eden, they were not alone. There were animals all around them.

Some only view animals as a source for food, or as tools to help man accomplish a task. God designed them for more than that.

> *And the Lord God said, it is not good that man should be alone; I will make a help meet for him. And out of the ground the LORD God formed every beast of the field, and every fowl of the air; and brought them unto Adam to see what he would call them: and whatsoever Adam called every living creature, that was the name thereof. And Adam gave names to all cattle, and to the fowl of the air, and to every beast of the field; but for Adam there was not found a help meet for him.*
>
> Genesis 2:18-20

When God created Adam, he said it was not good for man to be alone. After saying that, the Bible tells us God brought every animal that lived on the land, and in the air, to Adam. He let Adam name each of them. That was in direct response to man's need for companionship.

There was some level of companionship between man and animals in the Garden of Eden. Though animals do not replace the need for human companionship, some animals make great companions. They can provide mutually beneficial relationships.

In addition to Adam and Eve, and the animals, there was someone else in the Garden of Eden. His name was Lucifer. He was also called the Devil and Satan.

> *How art thou fallen from heaven, O Lucifer, son of the morning! how art thou cut down to the ground, which didst weaken the nations!* Isaiah 14:12
>
> *Thou hast been in Eden the garden of God; every precious stone was thy covering, the sardius, topaz, and*

the diamond, the beryl, the onyx, and the jasper, the sapphire, the emerald, and the carbuncle, and gold: the workmanship of thy tabrets and of thy pipes was prepared in thee in the day that thou wast created.
Ezekiel 28:13

And the great dragon was cast out, that old serpent, called the Devil, and Satan, which deceiveth the whole world: he was cast out into the earth, and his angels were cast out with him.
Revelation 12:9

The Devil used a serpent to trick Eve into disobeying God. Some are familiar with that event, but many miss some significant elements.

Fall of Adam and Eve
Woodcut by Julius Schnnorr von Carolsfeld (1794-1872)

And the serpent said unto the woman, Ye shall not surely die: For God doth know that in the day ye eat thereof, then your eyes shall be opened, and ye shall be as gods, knowing good and evil. And when the woman saw that the tree was good for food, and that it was pleasant to

the eyes, and a tree to be desired to make one wise, she took of the fruit thereof, and did eat, and he did eat.
Genesis 3:4-6

Notice in this encounter the serpent spoke to Eve. Have you ever considered the fact Eve had a conversation with a snake? That is very significant. What would you do if a snake started to speak to you? If that happened to me, I would be quite concerned. Yet, it does not appear Eve thought it was strange a snake could speak.

Is it possible snakes and other animals spoke in the garden? We will look at that significant aspect of that encounter in another chapter.

The next element from that encounter we need to consider is Adam and Eve disobeyed God and ate from the tree. When they did, what happened to them? Did they drop dead? No. We know Adam and Eve lived for many more years. So, what happened to the warning God gave them which said, *the day thou eatest therof, thou shalt surely die?*

Some theologians teach what God meant was, if they disobeyed Him and ate from the tree, they would *begin to die*. Notice their emphasis is on *begin to die.*

God did not say to them, the day they ate from that tree they would *begin to die.* He said they day they ate from that tree, they would *surely die.*

Whenever God says something will happen, it will happen. If God said the day Adam and Eve ate from the tree they would die, then the day they ate from the tree they died. So what happened?

When we think of someone dying, we usually think of physical death. That is the time when a body ceases to function, and the person is no longer alive. When a person dies physically they are separated from us. That type of death happens every day to people and animals.

The question, *where do we, or animals go when we die,* is often asked regarding that type of death. Apparently that is not the *death* God meant when He told Adam and Eve the day they ate from that one tree, they would die.

There is a different kind of death. In the Garden of Eden, God was talking about *spiritual death*. Some theologians think spiritual death means our spirit does not work, similar to how a physical body does not work when it dies. I believe they are wrong.

In Isaiah, God explains what spiritual death means.

But your iniquities have separated between you and your God, and your sins have hid his face from you, that he will not hear. Isaiah 59:2

Death means separation. When we die physically our spirit and soul are separated from our bodies. When we die spiritually our spirit is separated from God. Our spirit still works, it is just separated from God and cannot find fulfillment.

People who are spiritually dead can still do spiritual things, such as pray, read the Bible, or go to church. Some even love their neighbors but they are separated from the close intimate relationship God wants with them.

It is important to understand sin is doing, thinking, or saying anything contrary to what God wants us to do. Sin separates us from God and all the good He has for us. That separation is called spiritual death.

Behold, all souls are mine; as the soul of the father, so also the soul of the son is mine: the soul that sinneth, it shall die. Ezekiel 18:4

Spiritual death started in the Garden of Eden when Adam and Eve sinned. From that day, right to the present, everyone sins. We all willingly chose to do what we want instead of the wonderful things God wants us to do.

As it is written, There is none righteous, no, not one: There is none that understandeth, there is none that seeketh after God. They are all gone out of the way, they are together become unprofitable; there is none that doeth good, no, not one. Romans 3:10-13

For all have sinned and come short of the glory of God. Romans 3:23

As a result of our sin we die spiritually. Everyone sins and is spiritually dead. We are all separated from God.

For the wages of sin is death; but the gift of God is eternal life through Jesus Christ our Lord. Romans 6:23

The wages of sin is death. Wages are something we earn, something we deserve. The only way to pay for sin is death. When Adam and Eve sinned, they died spiritually. They were no longer innocent so they could not pay that price. They were separated from God. The only way to pay the price for their sin, and end that separation, was to have someone innocent physically die in their place.

Before Adam and Eve sinned, not one person or animal died. Death did not start until they sinned. Death is the ultimate penalty for sin.

The good news is God did not want man to remain separated. He provided a solution. Man needed a sinless sacrifice. God decided He would come to earth, become a man, and pay the price for our sin.

Until that day God provided a temporary solution. He had an innocent animal die for man's sin. Unlike humans, animals do not disobey God. They are sinless and innocent.

Bulls, goats, and lambs were the preferred sacrificial animals. Many people consider lambs to be an gentle, adorable animals. The idea of killing an innocent animal can seem cruel. It was a reminder of the awful price for sin and should have served as a deterrent.

The death of a sinless animal provided a covering (atonement) for sin. It was a foreshadowing of the day when the promised Savior of the world, the sinless Lamb of God, Jesus Christ, would come and die for all of us.

For the life of the flesh is in the blood: and I have given it to you upon the altar to make an atonement for your souls: for it is the blood that maketh an atonement for the soul. Leviticus 17:11

Illustration of Adam and Eve and Coats of Skin
From Medieval Latin Bible

For it is not possible that the blood of bulls and of goats should take away sins. Hebrews 10:4

Later in the Old Testament God reinforced this teaching. God instructed Abraham to take his only son Isaac and offer him as a sacrifice to God. Even though that did not make sense, Abraham obeyed God. Isaac did not know he was to be the sacrifice. He asked his father where was the lamb for the sacrifice? Abraham responded prophetically in faith.

And Abraham said, My son, God will provide himself a lamb for a burnt offering: so they went both of them together. Genesis 22:8

God did provide an animal for the sacrifice that day, but just as Abraham said, one day God would provide Himself as the perfect final sacrificial lamb. That was Jesus Christ.

When Jesus Christ began His earthly ministry, John the Baptist introduced Him as The lamb of God, which takes away the sins of the world.

The next day John seeth Jesus coming unto him, and saith, Behold the Lamb of God, which taketh away the sin of the world. John 1:29

A lamb could only provide a covering for one sin for one person or group of people. Jesus Christ, being God, was the only perfect final sacrifice for all people.

By the which will we are sanctified through the offering of the body of Jesus Christ once for all. Hebrews 10:10

One night, a religious leader named Nicodemus came to Jesus. He asked how he could have eternal life. He realized religion was not enough. He knew he was separated from God and needed new life.

Jesus answered, Verily, verily, I say unto thee, Except a man be born of water and of the Spirit, he cannot enter into the kingdom of God. That which is born of the flesh is flesh; and that which is born of the Spirit is spirit. Marvel not that I said unto thee, Ye must be born again. John 3:5-7

Jesus made it clear, physical birth is not enough. When our mother's water breaks and we come into this world, that is not enough for us to live a truly fulfilling life.

All humans are born in sin. We are separated from God. We all sin and need a spiritual rebirth. We need the separation to end between us and God. We need to be saved from our sins and need to be born again.

Jesus came and paid the price for our sins and provided a way for us to be saved. He loves us. He paid our debt and gave His life so we could have new life.

For God so loved the world, that he gave his only begotten Son, that whosoever believeth in him should not perish, but have everlasting life. For God sent not his Son into the world to condemn the world; but that the world through him might be saved. John 3:16-17

What do we need to do to end the separation and get new life? How can we be saved? You cannot offer an innocent animal in your place.

That if thou shalt confess with thy mouth the Lord Jesus, and shalt believe in thine heart that God hath raised him from the dead, thou shalt be saved. For with the heart man believeth unto righteousness; and with the mouth confession is made unto salvation. For the scripture saith, Whosoever believeth on him shall not be ashamed. For there is no difference between the Jew and the Greek: for the same Lord over all is rich unto all that call upon him. For whosoever shall call upon the name of the LORD shall be saved. Romans 10:9-13*

If you will believe the fact you are a sinner, and your sin has separated you from God, and understand you cannot save yourself, and believe Jesus paid the price for your sins, and will humbly call upon God and ask Him to save you, God will do that. You will be born again. He will give you new life. You will no longer be spiritually dead. Have you done that? If not, will you call upon Him now?

Though all humans need to be born again, it is important to understand an important fact. Though animals are affected by our sins in many ways, the Bible never says animals sin, nor does it say they are spiritually dead. Animals do not need to be born again.

We must understand, when Adam and Eve, our ancestors, choose to disobey God and sinned, their actions affected them and all their descendants, including you and me. That also affected all the animals living at that time and all their descendants.

Wherefore, as by one man sin entered into the world, and death by sin; and so death passed upon all men, for that all have sinned. Romans 5:11*

The sad truth is, the first animal to die, died as a sacrifice for man's sin. The good news is, that sacrifice provided an atonement for man's sin. An atonement is *a covering*. The sacrifice of that animal provided a spiritual covering for the sins of Adam and Eve as well as a physical covering for their bodies.

And almost all things are by the law purged with blood;

and without shedding this is no remission of sin.
Hebrews 9:22

Unto Adam also and to his wife did the LORD God make coats of skins, and clothed them.
Genesis 3:21

God does not like animals dying for our sin. God promised, one day He would put an end to all animal sacrifices by providing one of Adam and Eve's descendants to be a perfect sacrifice for sin. Until that day, a sinless blood sacrifice was required. For thousands of years, innocent, sinless animals died as an offering for man's sin.

When Jesus Christ came as the perfect Lamb of God, He died for our sins and put an end to the sacrifice of animals once and for all.

The next day John seeth Jesus coming unto him, and saith, Behold the Lamb of God, which taketh away the sin of the world.
John 1:29

When John the Baptist introduced Jesus, the promised descendent of Adam and Eve, he called Him *the Lamb of God, which taketh away the sin of the world.*

Just like a lamb, Jesus was sinless. He never sinned, so He could die in our place. If Jesus was just a man, then He could only die for one of us. The fact, He is both sinless man and Eternal God, means He could die for all of us.

Then said I, Lo, I come (in the volume of the book it is written of me,) to do thy will, O God. Above when he said, Sacrifice and offering and burnt offerings and offering for sin thou wouldest not, neither hadst pleasure therein; which are offered by the law; Then said he, Lo, I come to do thy will, O God. He taketh away the first, that he may establish the second. By the which will we are sanctified through the offering of the body of Jesus Christ once for all.
Hebrews 10:7-10

The requirement that an innocent animal had to die for sin did not deter men from sinning. God never liked the fact animals had to die for man's sins. It was the sinful choices man willingly made which caused all those innocent animals to die. When Jesus came, as the Lamb of God, and died for our sins, no more blood sacrifice was required. He died once for all.

Adam and Eve's sin did not just cause animals to die as a sacrifice for man's sin. Animals also started to die because Adam and Eve's sin brought the curse of death upon the world. Prior to their sin both man and animals lived without fear of death. Not a single animal died until Adam and Eve sinned. Once they sinned, the endless cycle of death began. Death started with that first animal who died to be a sacrifice for sin. It then continued as the curse fell and death covered the world. Disease and age were a consequence of the curse. That cause many animals to die.

Some people assume Adam and Eve ate meat because their son Cain raised sheep. That is only an assumption. Sheep can be used for food, but many people raise sheep primarily for their wool.

The Bible seems to teach Adam and Eve did not eat any animals. It was not until after the flood, more than 600 years after creation, that God specifically said man could eat animals. It is also likely, animals did not eat each other until after the flood.

From man's fall, until the day the flood covered the world, man became more and more sinful. That had negative effects on animals. When Adam and Eve sinned, the ground was cursed. Man had to work hard to make a living. That meant man had less time for rest and relaxation. That had an effect on how much time they could spend with the animals.

Some people have little interaction with animals, some have significantly more. I did not have a lot of interaction with animals while I was growing up. I was born in New York City and grew up in the suburbs. The only animal, which lived near me were dogs. I rarely saw a few cats. I never saw any racoons or squirrels where I lived. There weren't any farms near us, and no one had cows, horses, pigs, or chickens. I only saw those animals on television or when we travelled.

My wife grew up on a farm in Pennsylvania. They had

cows, pigs and chickens. White Tailed Deer and Black Bears lived in the woods on their property. They had dogs and cats, but not like the ones where I grew up. Instead of yippy spoiled Toy Poodles, like my mother had, they had working dogs like Beagles and German Shepherds.

When I visited my wife's family farm, I was thrilled to see animals close up, instead of on a television. I discovered Many of those animals had distinctive personalities. Most animals do, we are usually too busy to take the time and notice.

I did not have a conversation with any animals, the way Eve did with the Serpent, or as Balaam did with his ass, but over the years, the ones I paid attention to responded.

Many times people get so busy with life they have little time for meaningful interactions with animals. Often sin complicates our lives and pushes away any such interaction. Both we and the animals miss out.

Sin is such a problem that man's selfishness and sinfulness led to the extinction of some animals.

Man's continuing sinfulness has an on-going effect on many animals. It is so sad many animals are abused or neglected every day. Few animals experience the truly meaningful relationships with man which God designed them to have. Sin hurts both man and animals.

One time sin got so bad, it resulted in a world changing event which effected every man and animal.

Questions for Thought or Discussion
Chapter 3
The Sin Problem

1. What is sin?

2. How did sin affect animals?

3. What was the penalty of Adam and Eve's sin?

4. Why could Adam and Eve not pay the penalty for their sin?

5. Do Animals sin?

6. How was the penalty for sin paid?

7. Why is Jesus called the Lamb of God?

Chapter 4

Animals & The Worldwide Flood

And GOD saw that the wickedness of man was great in the earth, and that every imagination of the thoughts of his heart was only evil continually. And it repented the LORD that he had made man on the earth, and it grieved him at his heart. And the LORD said, I will destroy man whom I have created from the face of the earth; both man, and beast, and the creeping thing, and the fowls of the air; for it repenteth me that I have made them.
Genesis 6:5-7

The earth also was corrupt before God, and the earth was filled with violence. And God looked upon the earth, and, behold, it was corrupt; for all flesh had corrupted his way upon the earth. And God said unto Noah, The end of all flesh is come before me; for the earth is filled with violence through them; and, behold, I will destroy them with the earth. Make thee an ark of gopher wood; rooms shalt thou make in the ark, and shalt pitch it within and without with pitch.   Genesis 6:11-14

And, behold, I, even I, do bring a flood of waters upon the earth, to destroy all flesh, wherein is the breath of life, from under heaven; and every thing that is in the earth shall die. And, behold, I, even I, do bring a flood of waters upon the earth, to destroy all flesh, wherein is the breath of life, from under heaven; and every thing that is in the earth shall die. But with thee will I establish my covenant; and thou shalt come into the ark, thou, and thy sons, and thy wife, and thy sons' wives with thee. And of every living thing of all flesh, two of every sort shalt thou bring into the ark, to keep them alive with thee; they shall be male and female. Of fowls after their kind, and of cattle after their kind, of every creeping thing of the earth after his kind, two of every sort shall come unto thee, to keep them alive.   Genesis 6:17-20

And the waters prevailed exceedingly upon the earth; and all the high hills, that were under the whole heaven, were covered. Fifteen cubits upward did the waters prevail; and the mountains were covered. And all flesh died that moved upon the earth, both of fowl, and of cattle, and of beast, and of every creeping thing that creepeth upon the earth, and every man: All in whose nostrils was the breath of life, of all that was in the dry land, died. And every living substance was destroyed which was upon the face of the ground, both man, and cattle, and the creeping things, and the fowl of the heaven; and they were destroyed from the earth: and Noah only remained alive, and they that were with him in the ark. Genesis 7:19-23

Like many people today, our ancestors turned their backs on God. Their sin became so great it corrupted the entire world. As a result of their sin, God sent a worldwide flood to cleanse the world and give it a new beginning. That event changed the world and had a direct impact on man and animals.

Before the flood man and animals lived for an exceptionally long time. There is a scientific explanation for that. When God created this world, He did something special. He placed a protective water barrier, called the *firmament* around the earth.

And God said, Let there be a firmament in the midst of the waters, and let it divide the waters from the waters. And God made the firmament, and divided the waters which were under the firmament from the waters which were above: and it was so. Genesis 1:6-7

It appears that barrier stopped much harmful radiation and some ultra-violet light from penetrating the atmosphere. With those harmful elements filtered out, most animals, as well as humans lived a very long time. The entire earth was like a greenhouse. The fossil record confirms tropical vegetation grew all over the world.

Some creatures, such as reptiles, grow until they die. Though their growth rate slows down, the older a reptile gets the larger they grow. The protective barrier enabled some reptiles to grow enormously large. The fossil record attests to that. We call them *dinosaurs*.

Alligators and crocodiles grow about one foot a year. One time I saw an alligator which was almost twenty years old. It was fifteen feet long. Imagine how large one would grow if it could live for more than one hundred years.

In order to justify their theory of evolution, which includes the development of new species, evolutionists teach the world is billions of years old. They teach dinosaurs came into existence millions of years ago and died many years before man ever came into existence and lived on earth. To support their theory, they place the evolutionary development of different species in clearly defined layers, comprising millions of years.

The Bible contradicts that teaching. The Bible teaches God created all species in just one week and that they lived at the same time. The protective canopy God place around the earth, prior to the flood, can account for some species attaining enormous size.

The fossil record attests to tropical vegetation all around the world, it also attests to various species, which evolutionists place in different ages, actually living at the same time. Unlike the fanciful textbook illustrations purporting the homogenous evolutionary layers, much of the actual fossil record is polystratic. Multiple species from various supposed ages are found mixed together, with some fossils crossing through various layers.

A good example of that is at Dinosaur National Park in Vernal, Utah. The actual fossil record there reveals intermixed species laid down by a cataclysmic event involving water, such as the Bible describes.

Contrary to what evolutions teach, most creationists believe man and dinosaurs lived at the same time. There are numerous fossil records which included human and dinosaur footprints together.

Both man and animals had extremely long lifespans until the protective barrier was removed during the world-wide flood in Noah's day. The windows of heaven opened, and the water came pouring down.

In the six hundredth year of Noah's life, in the second month, the seventeenth day of the month, the same day were all the fountains of the great deep broken up, and the windows of heaven were opened. And the rain was upon the earth forty days and forty nights.

Genesis 7:11-12

The Entry into the Ark
Genesis chap. VII

Entry into the Ark
Engraving from Bible Published by Hubbards, 1870

God loves man and animals. God had Noah build an ark. On that ark God saved representatives from every species. There were at least two of every species and seven of some.

And the LORD said unto Noah, Come thou and all thy house into the ark; for thee have I seen righteous before

> *me in this generation. Of every clean beast thou shalt take to thee by sevens, the male and his female: and of beasts that are not clean by two, the male and his female. Of fowls also of the air by sevens, the male and the female; to keep seed alive upon the face of all the earth. For yet seven days, and I will cause it to rain upon the earth forty days and forty nights; and every living substance that I have made will I destroy from off the face of the earth.* Genesis 7:1-4

The fact the Bible says Noah took at least two of every animal on the ark, would mean Noah took dinosaurs on the ark. That caused some evolutionists to mock creationists and say, how could Noah fit dinosaurs on the ark? The answer to that is simple. He took the younger smaller ones. Most dinosaurs were not really big. It is estimated the average size of a dinosaur was the size of a chicken.

After the flood, the world changed. There were vast geographic upheavals. The landscape of the earth changed drastically, valleys lowered, mountains were raised.

> *Who laid the foundations of the earth, that it should not be removed for ever. Thou coveredst it with the deep as with a garment: the waters stood above the mountains. At thy rebuke they fled; at the voice of thy thunder they hasted away. They go up by the mountains; they go down by the valleys unto the place which thou hast founded for them. Thou hast set a bound that they may not pass over; that they turn not again.* Psalm 104:5-9

When the animals came off the ark they dispersed and spread around the world. As they spread out, the continents shifted. Some areas like Australia and Japan, as well as many islands had land bridges which shifted or disappeared. That resulted in some species being protected from certain predators, and kept them from going extinct.

The removal of the protective barrier had a drastic effect on the lifespan of man and reptiles. Both are especially susceptible to radiation and cosmic rays. Many reptiles gradually went extinct. Few grew to monstrous sizes any more. Some became the subject of legends.

Not only did lifespans significantly decrease after the flood it appears something else changed significantly. In the Garden of Eden, before the fall, man and animals were all herbivores. That means they did not eat any meat. According to the Bible, originally all man and animals were herbivores and only ate plants and fruits.

> *And God said, Behold, I have given you every herb bearing seed, which is upon the face of all the earth, and every tree, in the which is the fruit of a tree yielding seed; to you it shall be for meat. And to every beast of the earth, and to every fowl of the air, and to every thing that creepeth upon the earth, wherein there is life, I have given every green herb for meat: and it was so.*
> Genesis 1:29-30

It is an undisputed fact, a number of animals eat other animals. Just because some animals are better suited for eating other animals does not mean they do or always did.

One day the Bible says some predators will no longer eat other animals. It speaks of a future time, known as the *Millennium.* That will be a one thousand year period of peace on earth. Animals, which are usually carnivorous, will live peacefully together with animals which would normally be their prey. It says even lions will eat straw.

> *The wolf also shall dwell with the lamb, and the leopard shall lie down with the kid; and the calf and the young lion and the fatling together; and a little child shall lead them.* Isaiah 11:6

> *The wolf and the lamb shall feed together, and the lion shall eat straw like the bullock: and dust shall be the serpent's meat. They shall not hurt nor destroy in all my holy mountain.* Isaiah 65:25

It is very possible neither man nor beast ate other animals until after the flood, just as animals will not eat each other during the Millennium.

The Bible says, after the flood, God told Noah of two significant changes in the new world.

> *And God blessed Noah and his sons, and said unto them,*

Be fruitful, and multiply, and replenish the earth. And the fear of you and the dread of you shall be upon every beast of the earth, and upon every fowl of the air, upon all that moveth upon the earth, and upon all the fishes of the sea; into your hand are they delivered. Every moving thing that liveth shall be meat for you; even as the green herb have I given you all things.

Genesis 9:1-3

The first thing which would be different, after the flood, was all animals would have a fear and dread of man. It appears animals did not fear man before the flood. Imagine man and animals living peacefully together. That must have been wonderful.

Perhaps God gave animals that fear of man to protect them knowing man would follow sin again and be selfish and not consider the well-being of others, including animals.

The second thing God told Noah would change was the fact animals could now become part of man's diet. Notice God used the words *shall be meat for you*. He did not say *are* or *will continue to be*. The use of the word *shall*, makes a very strong case that man would start having meat in their diet. I would not be surprised many animals would avoid man after hearing that news.

Both man and animals were directly affected by the worldwide flood. God preserved both. He made sure all species were saved.

The sad thing is, after the flood, man quickly and selfishly embraced sin. That has hurt both man and animals. It is going to get worse. The Bible warns us before Jesus returns, the world will once again be filled with sin as it was in Noah's day and will deserve judgment. That has become a disappointing reality in the world.

And as it was in the days of Noe, so shall it be also in the days of the Son of man. They did eat, they drank, they married wives, they were given in marriage, until the day that Noe entered into the ark, and the flood came, and destroyed them all. Luke 17:26-27

Questions for Thought or Discussion
Chapter 4
Animals & the Worldwide Flood

1. What were lifespans like before the worldwide flood? What role did the firmament play in that?

2. What affect did the longer lifespans have on reptiles?

3. What happened to the earth's geography as a result of, and from events after, the flood?

4. Why did God have Noah build an ark? What animals went on the ark?

5. How did man's diet change after the flood?

Chapter 5

God Cares for Animals

He giveth to the beast his food, and to the young ravens which cry. Psalm 147:9

The beast of the field shall honour me, the dragons and the owls: because I give waters in the wilderness, and rivers in the desert, to give drink to my people, my chosen. Isaiah 43:20

It is important we understand how much God cares for animals. It may not seem like that needs to be said, but I think it does.

The Nativity
Engraving by Gustave Dore (1823-1883)

Animals were present the day Jesus Christ, God the Son left Heaven to become a man. He was born of the Virgin Mary, in a stable, and placed in a manger (a feeding trough for animals).

And she brought forth her firstborn son, and wrapped him in swaddling clothes, and laid him in a manger; because there was no room for them in the inn.
Luke 2:7

As Jesus entered the city of Jerusalem the week before He was crucified for our sins, He entered the city with two animals.

Entry of Jesus into Jerusalem
Engraving by Gustave Dore (1825-1883)

And when they drew nigh unto Jerusalem, and were come to Bethphage, unto the mount of Olives, then sent Jesus two disciples, Saying unto them, Go into the village over against you, and straightway ye shall find an ass tied, and a colt with her: loose them, and bring them unto me. And if any man say ought unto you, ye shall say, The Lord hath need of them; and straightway he will send them. All this was done, that it might be fulfilled which was spoken by the prophet, saying, Tell ye the daughter of Sion, Behold, thy King cometh unto thee, meek, and sitting upon an ass, and a colt the foal of an ass. And the disciples went, and did as Jesus commanded them, And brought the ass, and the colt, and put on them their clothes.   Matthew 17:1-7

It is obvious God cares for animals. Someone once told me, *God must like animals, He made so many of them.* There are more than sixty different types of animals specifically mentioned in the Bible. Many of those animals are found all over the world.

God Creating the Animals
Painting by Raphael (1483-1520)

I find it interesting one animal not mentioned in the Bible is the cat. Cats played an important life in the Egyptian culture. The Egyptians considered them magical creatures. Cats were treated better than slaves.

Though some people care for animals it is a sad thing many do not. Many live their lives focused on themselves, They are the center of their own world. They put themselves first, then others. Many provide no time to care for animals.

I believe if people understood how much God cares for animals, perhaps they would show them more care.

Some feel sad when they see commercials on television which show animals suffering. It is sad many people neglect animals and few take meaningful action to help.

Some show care toward their own pets but very few take purposeful time out of their day to express love and concern to other animals. Perhaps they do not see the value in that.

Many people do not greet other humans when they see them. Especially ones they do not know. I try to do that because I know it can brighten someone's day. People have told me they appreciate that. Even fewer people greet animals or smile at them as they pass by. Animals respond to kindness, yet many animals never receive it.

I feel sad every time I see an animal look sad. It upsets me when I see others neglecting or hurting animals.

I also feel sad when I see an animal lying dead by the side of the road. I often wonder if it was a mother and if it left behind little ones who will miss it.

The Sparrow
Engraving from Bible Animals , 1883

Are not five sparrows sold for two farthings, and not one of them is forgotten before God? Luke 12:6

Does it make you sad to see an animal die? There are millions and millions of sparrows. They are a bird viewed as valueless by many. Perhaps that is the way others view you and me. Yet, God knows when even one sparrow dies.

God cares for animals. He shows that in many ways. One reason we know God loves human beings is because He created us. We must remember He also loves animals and created them.

Some may think the only reason God created animals was to provide food for man. That is wrong. Though many today get their food from animals, it appears man did not eat any animal until more than 600 years after God created man. Now, centuries later, though some animals provide food for mankind, man only derives food from an exceedingly small fraction of the vast species of animals.

I like many animals. I am thankful there are so many different kinds. I love the unique differences between them. I am sure God feels the same way because He is the one who created them. They did not evolve over the course of millions of years, from some primordial soup. God purposefully created them in just two days. He made them in all shapes and sizes. From the tiny mouse to the mighty Tyrannosaurus Rex. God purposefully made every animal.

God loves animas so much and made many varieties. He even made some look like some creatures He made to live with Him in Heaven. Some heavenly extraterrestrial beings look like lions, oxen, eagles, and horses. We will look at that in another chapter.

Animals make the world a beautiful and better place. That is the way God designed things. He not only created animals, but showed how much He cares for them by creating a beautiful world to fulfill all their needs. It has many wonderful places, suited exactly for them.

> *Therefore I say unto you, Take no thought for your life, what ye shall eat, or what ye shall drink; nor yet for your body, what ye shall put on. Is not the life more than meat, and the body than raiment? Behold the fowls of the air: for they sow not, neither do they reap, nor gather into barns; yet your heavenly Father feedeth them. Are ye not much better than they?*
> Matthew 6:25-26

God not only provides a beautiful place where animals

can live, He also provides food for them.

> *And to every beast of the earth, and to every fowl of the air, and to every thing that creepeth upon the earth, wherein there is life, I have given every green herb for meat: and it was so.*   Genesis 1:30

All animals were originally herbivores. That means they all ate plants, not meat. Evolutionists dispute that. They say, if all animals were herbivores why do some have sharp claws and teeth? They believe those features evolved to help some animals eat others.

Just because an animal has claws and sharp teeth does not mean they must eat other animals. The Panda Bear is a perfect example of that. The Panda Bear has very sharp teeth and claws yet is an herbivore. It uses its claws to help climb trees and uses its sharp teeth to eat bamboo.

Koala Bears also have sharp teeth, so do Kangaroos. Neither are meat eating carnivores. Koala Bears are very slow, so even if they did eat meat, they would have a hard time catching it. Kangaroos, on the other hand are fast and strong. Humans should be glad Kangaroos are not carnivorous.

Early Artist Conception of Tyrannosaurus Rex
Charles R. Knight, 1919

The Tyrannosaurus Rex is another example of an animal with very sharp teeth. Like all other animals it was an herbivore at first. It may have been such until they went extinct. Most movies portray them as carnivorous predators. The problem with that is the fossil record shows the Tyrannosaurus' teeth are not set very deeply in its jaw. If they were to try to bite and tear apart another animal, the ensuing struggle would probably cause their teeth to fall out. Perhaps if they had special reinforced dentures they could have been carnivores. They also had short arms which made it difficult for them to grab or hold any potential prey.

Another way God shows He cares for animals is He made man to help watch over them.

> *And God said, Let us make man in our image, after our likeness: and let them have dominion over the fish of the sea, and over the fowl of the air, and over the cattle, and over all the earth, and over every creeping thing that creepeth upon the earth.* Genesis 1:26

God gave man the responsibility to take care of animals. The word *dominion* in this passage is different than our modern conception of that word. Here it means man was given oversight to make sure animals were taken care of. Some take that responsibility seriously, many do not. This is an area where man as a whole has done a bad job.

> *A righteous man regardeth the life of his beast: but the tender mercies of the wicked are cruel.* Proverbs 12:10

A righteous man, one who honors God by doing what is right, will treat animals well. The problem is too many do not honor God in their lives. Some evidence that by being cruel to animals.

Man's sinful behavior always impacts animals. When men ignore God's directives and live for themselves they not only hurt themselves but other people and animals.

Man often neglects his God-given responsibility to take care of animals, as a result many animals are hurt or exploited. Some have needlessly gone extinct.

Questions for Thought or Discussion
Chapter 5
God Cares for Animals

1. At what two significant events in the life of Christ were animals present?

2. What is one reason many people do not take time to show care or concern for animals?

3. What can we learn about God from sparrows?

4. How does God provide for animals?

5. What does it mean when we say all animals were originally herbivores?

6. What does the Bible mean when it says man should have dominion over animals?

Chapter 6

Animals Have a Sensitivity to God

The heavens declare the glory of God; and the firmament sheweth his handywork. Day unto day uttereth speech, and night unto night sheweth knowledge. There is no speech nor language, where their voice is not heard. Psalm 19:1-3

For the wrath of God is revealed from heaven against all ungodliness and unrighteousness of men, who hold the truth in unrighteousness; Because that which may be known of God is manifest in them; for God hath shewed it unto them. For the invisible things of him from the creation of the world are clearly seen, being understood by the things that are made, even his eternal power and Godhead; so that they are without excuse: Because that, when they knew God, they glorified him not as God, neither were thankful; but became vain in their imaginations, and their foolish heart was darkened. Romans 1:18-21

The vast universe above us, and the world around us, clearly show us the great God, whom we cannot physically see, truly and undeniably exists. Both man and animals recognize that. Too many humans choose to ignore that. They suppress the truth and deny their Creator. That negatively affects the way they think, feel, and act. That has a direct impact on them, on others, and on animals.

Unlike humans, animals never deny God. They have a sensitivity to their Creator. They do as God tells them. In the First Book of Kings, chapter 13, there was a man of God who was sent to give a warning to King Jeroboam. God told him to deliver the message and then return home without stopping to eat or drink. As he headed home an old prophet wanted to see him so the prophet sent one of his sons to the man of God telling him the Lord said he should come see the prophet. That was a lie. The man of God should have obeyed what God clearly said to him, but he went to see the old prophet and ate with him. He disobeyed the clear word of God. As a result God sent a lion to kill him. The lion responded to God and killed the prophet. The lion did not act as a wild lion normally would. It did not eat the prophet nor kill the prophet's animal. It stood guard over the prophet's body.

The Disobedient Prophet Slain by the Lion
Engraving by Gustave Dore (1832-1883)

And when he was gone, a lion met him by the way, and slew him: and his carcase was cast in the way, and the ass stood by the carcase. And, behold, men passed by, and saw the carcase cast in the way, and the lion standing by the carcase: and they came and told it in the city where the old prophet dwelt. And when the prophet that brought him back from the way heard thereof, he said, It is the man of God, who was disobedient unto the word of the LORD: therefore the LORD hath delivered him unto the lion, which hath torn him, and slain him, according to the word of the LORD, which he spake unto him. And he spake to his sons, saying, Saddle me the ass. And they saddled him and he went and found his carcase cast in the way, and the ass and the lion standing by the carcase: the lion had not eaten the carcase, nor torn the ass.   1 Kings 13:24-28

When the prophet Daniel was held captive by the Babylonians he was thrown into a lion's den as punishment for his faith. Normally those lions ate whoever were thrown in the den with them. When Daniel was thrown into that lion's den the lions obeyed God and did not eat Daniel.

Daniel in the Lion's Den
Engraving by Gustave Dore (1832-1883)

Before man sinned animals lived in a perfect paradise. When our ancestors, Adam and Eve, choose to disobey God and sinned, their sin affected them and all animals. Now man and animals live in a world corrupted by sin.

Both man and animals existence became a struggle because of our sin. They had to endure that for thousands of years. The Bible says they groan in pain waiting for the *adoption* to take place.

> *For we know that the whole creation groaneth and travaileth in pain together until now. And not only they, but ourselves also, which have the firstfruits of the Spirit, even we ourselves groan within ourselves, waiting for the adoption, to wit, the redemption of our body.* Romans 8:22-23

What is this *adoption* the animals look forward to? It is not speaking of you going to an animal shelter and adopting an animal, though that is a nice thing to do. In the Bible the adoption it is talking about is also called the *redemption of the body*. It takes place in the future when Jesus Christ returns. It is when our sinful earthly bodies are transformed into perfect heavenly bodies which will never get sick or die.

To better understand this you need to understand the difference between the *penalty*, the *power*, and the *presence* of sin. Those affect every one of us.

> *And He is the propitiation for our sins: and not for ours only, but also for the sins of the whole world.* 1 John 2:2

There is a *penalty* for sin. Sin separates us from a relationship with God and from His blessings. It also separates us from others. It causes great hurt and harm. We cannot payoff that penalty.

When Jesus died on the cross, He paid the price for the sins of the whole world. He provided a means for us to be saved from the *penalty* of sin. That becomes a reality in our lives the moment we accept His gift of eternal life.

> *But as many as received him, to them gave He power to*

become the sons of God, even to them that believe on his name. John 1:12

The problem is, even if you are saved, though the penalty for your sins is paid you still live in a sinful world with a sinful body and a sinful mind. Every day you live you must deal with the *power* and *presence* of sin. Too often we do not deal well with those. The *power* of sin and the *presence* of sin often cause us to hurt ourselves and others, including animals.

Behold, I shew you a mystery; We shall not all sleep, but we shall all be changed, In a moment, in the twinkling of an eye, at the last trump: for the trumpet shall sound, and the dead shall be raised incorruptible, and we shall be changed. For this corruptible must put on incorruption, and this mortal must put on immortality. So when this corruptible shall have put on incorruption, and this mortal shall have put on immortality, then shall be brought to pass the saying that is written, Death is swallowed up in victory. O death, where is thy sting? O grave, where is thy victory? The sting of death is sin; and the strength of sin is the law. But thanks be to God, which giveth us the victory through our Lord Jesus Christ. 1 Corinthians 15:-51-*57*

We need to learn how to deal with the *power of sin*. Sin is powerful and is all around us. We must recognize that. It is always tempting us and trying to get us to do wrong. If we do not control sin, it will control us.

There hath no temptation taken you but such as is common to man: but God is faithful, who will not suffer you to be tempted above that ye are able; but will with the temptation also make a way to escape, that ye may be able to bear it. 1 Corinthians 10:13

I can do all things through Christ which strengtheneth me. Philippians 4:13

As long as we live on Earth, sin will always be around us. Though it is immensely powerful God can help you overcome the *power* of sin if you ask Him.

Ultimately, when Jesus returns, He will destroy the *power* of sin. On that day, He will also deliver us from the *presence* of sin. There will no longer be any sin around to give us any trouble. He will give us new perfected bodies. That is called the *redemption of the body*, the adoption.

> *For the flesh lusteth against the Spirit, and the Spirit against the flesh: and these are contrary the one to the other: so that ye cannot do the things that ye would.*
> Galatians 5:17

You cannot overcome the power of sin on your own. Instead of acknowledging we have a problem with sin, and seeking help from God to deal with the power of sin, most people try to live life in their own strength. That does not work out too well. When we live in our own strength we fail.

Too many times people not only have a problem with the power of sin but willingly disobey God. It is usually for selfish reasons. Some people purposefully hurt others.

Animals do not disobey God. Though some animals may hurt people, unlike some people, animals do not hurt people just to hurt them. Unlike humans, animals are not cruel. Unless they are hungry, suffering from a disease, or protecting their families, animals do not usually hurt people or one another.

Sometimes our selfishness not only hurts us but carelessly destroys the food source for some animals.

> *How do the beasts groan! the herds of cattle are perplexed, because they have no pasture; yea, the flocks of sheep are made desolate.*
> Joel 1:18

Animals do not sin and do not succumb to the *power* of sin, but they experience the harmful consequences of the *presence* of sin and the *power* sin through humans. When animals suffer, as a result of our actions, the Bible says they call out to God. That is something we should do.

> *The beasts of the field cry also unto thee: for the rivers of waters are dried up, and the fire hath devoured the pastures of the wilderness.*
> Joel 1:20

Animals show their sensitivity to God in another way. They praise Him. God appreciates that. It would be nice if more people praised God.

> *Let the heaven and earth praise him, the seas, and every thing that moveth therein.*   Psalm 69:34

> *Praise the LORD from the earth, ye dragons, and all deeps.*   Psalm 148:7

The Bible even says dragons praise God.

Sometimes I wonder why God puts up with us. Too often, we do not honor Him and praise Him as we should. I also wonder why animals put up with us. It seems they should all get together and try to put an end to the way we hurt them, our world, and ourselves. I believe one reason they do not do that is because they have a sensitivity to God.

It would be nice if we all were more sensitive to God, like the animals, and wanted to please Him.

Questions for Thought or Discussion
Chapter 6
Animals Have a Sensitivity to God

1. The universe above us, and around us, clearly show us there is a great God. How do many humans respond to that?

2. Do animals deny God?

3. What was unique about the way the lion dealt with the disobedient prophet in 1 Kings 13?

4. What was unique about how the lions behaved when Daniel was thrown in a den with them?

5. What does the Bible say the animals *groan* looking forward to?

6. What is the difference between the penalty, power, and presence of sin?

Chapter 7

Animals Have Something to Say

We know the first woman, Eve, encountered a taking snake in the Garden of Eden. Have you ever met a talking animal? I mean one who speaks your language?

When I was younger there was a television show called *Mr. Ed.* It featured a talking horse named, Mr. Ed. I loved that show. It looked like that horse could speak. I was disappointed later when I learned it was just a gimmick.

That show was inspired by an enjoyable series of comedic movies featuring Donald O'Connor and *Francis the Talking Mule*. I discovered the mule who played Francis could not really talk, but the idea of a talking mule did appeal to many people.

One time when I was in England I visited one of the places where the movie *Dr. Doolittle,* with Rex Harrison, was filmed. In that film, Dr. Doolittle could talk with the animals, and they spoke with him, though they did not use his language. That was fiction but it was enjoyable.

I will never forget the time I encountered an animal which spoke my language. While visiting a friend, I heard someone talking in the other room. It sounded like two people were having a conversation. I finally asked who was talking. My friend took me to the other room and introduced me to his landlord's Myna Bird.

I said *hello* to the bird, and the bird said *hello* back to me. It spoke as clearly as a person.

I was impressed and tried to have a conversation with the bird. My friend told me you really cannot have a conversation with that bird. He said it only mimics what it hears. He said that bird could mimic almost anyone in that house. It even mimicked conversations between two different people using two different voices. He said that was what the bird was doing when I heard him speak. I later learned he was wrong about that bird, it could do more.

Most agree it would be unusual to encounter an animal which spoke your language, especially one you could have a meaningful conversation with. In spite of that, here are some important truths you need to understand.

Just because an animal does not speak your language, does not mean it does not have something to say. You must understand most animals talk. Some appear to be silent, but most talk in some way. They often talk with each other. Some appear to have their own language.

Some animals try to talk with people, but many do not listen. Some try to tell people when they are hungry or when they want to go out. Some try to let people know when they are afraid or happy. They probably try to talk with you. Do you listen?

The Bible teaches all animals have a body, a spirit, and a soul. The soul enables them to communicate with those around them. Having a soul means they have a mind, emotions and will. Animals think, feel, and make decisions. They may not think about many things humans think about. They do not face some of decisions we have to make but they do have to think and make decisions.

Some animals, who live inside, have to decide if they will relieve themselves inside or outside. They often try to let you know which decision they made. Sometimes people do not listen and suffer the consequences.

Just like you and me, some animals do not make good choices. And like some people, some animals make very good choices.

Some animals may seem to be as *wise as a professor*. Wait, I met some professors who are not very wise. Maybe we could say some are *as wise as an owl*.

Just like some people, animals can be quite cunning. Some try to manipulate things to get their way. When they do that we say they are as *wise as a politician*. Right? No. We should not insult animals that way. Maybe we could say *they are wise as a fox*.

Animals also have a will. If you tell an animal to go outside it must decide if it will do what you said. Some animals can be very stubborn, just like some people. Some can be as *stubborn as a Baptist*. Oh wait, I am a Baptist, and some Baptists I know are very stubborn, but the saying is, they are as *stubborn as a mule.*

Now back to the idea that animals have something to say. Some animals try to have conversations with those around them. Many people do not listen to animals, few pay close attention. Those who do often have great relationships with animals.

Scientists discovered some animals can learn sign language. Sign language is a form of language used by the Deaf and Hearing Impaired, I am Hearing Impaired and learned sign language. Through behavioral studies, and with much hard work, some scientists had success with apes learning many signs. Studies show people can also learn sign language too. Some people can learn many signs, most will not even try. Some animals sign better than most humans.

Many times do animals try to talk with you. Have you noticed? Have you ever walked by a house or car and had a dog bark at you? That was the dog trying to communicate with you.

Many times when animals try to communicate with us we ignore them, just like we ignore some people.

When you respond to an animal, who tries to communicate with you, it will often respond. If you are nice it will usually respond in a nice way. If you are mean it will often back away or may respond in a mean way to you.

Years ago my parents belonged to the *International Fan Travel Trailer Club*. That club consisted of people who owned travel trailers manufactured by the *Fan Trailer Company*. As part of that club we went to state, regional and national rallies. We travelled around the country and visited many nice places that way. Many people in that club owned dogs.

I will never forget one night we were sitting around in a

campground with a group of people from the trailer club. One member had two poodles with them. One of the other members present that night did not like dogs. He said something unkind to one of the dogs, in a very coarse way, and swatted at him. That dog backed away in fear.

As the conversation shifted, I watched as that dog slowly made its way around to the back of that person's chair. It then lifted its leg and relieved itself, using that person as a tree. That dog responded to the unkind way it was treated, just as some of us respond to people who treat us unkindly.

I am sure some of you had your own interesting experiences of animals responding to unkind people.

Some may not realize animals can have strong feelings just like you and me. I saw that when I was growing up on Long Island. We had an dog we named Pepsi. We gave her that name because her coat looked like the two colors you got when you quickly poured Pepsi Cola in a cup.

Pepsi liked to run around the neighborhood, even when she was not supposed to. She especially loved to run up to people, jump up on them to say hello, and then give them a nice wet friendly lick.

One of our neighbors, who lived directly across the street, was not very nice. He did not like dogs. One day Pepsi got out and decided that neighbor needed a friendly greeting. She ran right over to him and jumped up on him to share her kindness. He did not appreciate that.

All of a sudden I heard a loud thud and then a desperate *Yelp!* He hit Pepsi so hard she flew across his lawn.

I was shocked. So was Pepsi. She lay there for a moment then stumbled to her feet and ran quickly back to our front door and into our house.

After that incident my parents told us to be extra careful to make sure Pepsi did not get out. We did our best to comply with that. I watched as week after week, and month after month, passed. All that time Pepsi sat at the front window looking across the street.

Finally, after a few years, that neighbor decided to move. I am sure Pepsi watched the moving van arrive and leave. I believe that neighbor locked his house for one final time and headed to his car. As he did, Pepsi made a lunge for the front door and managed to get out.

I watched as she ran directly across the street. I saw a look of fear come across that neighbor's face as Pepsi approached. It appeared she did not forget their encounter from years ago. This time instead of jumping up and giving him a friendly lick, she ran over and bit him in the leg. Before he could hit her, she ran back to the house looking very satisfied. I was amazed at Pepsi's actions.

When my parents moved to Connecticut, Pepsi went with them. When I visited them I often saw Pepsi go to the front door. She would stand there wagging her tail, looking at the door. When someone finally paid attention to her, she made a sound which sounded like, *wanna woh owt!* I think she was trying to say, *want to go out.* I was not the only one who heard her say that.

Over the years I had many conversations with animals. Most consisted of words on my part and *woofs* and *purrs* from them. In all those encounters, we had a meaningful connection, but I never met an animal I had a two-way conversation with in my language.

The Bible says animals praise and glorify God. They may not use our words, but they do it.

> *Praise the LORD from the earth, ye dragons, and all deeps: Fire, and hail; snow, and vapour; stormy wind fulfilling his word: Mountains, and all hills; fruitful trees, and all cedars: Beasts, and all cattle; creeping things, and flying fowl: Kings of the earth, and all people; princes, and all judges of the earth: Both young men, and maidens; old men, and children: Let them praise the name of the LORD: for his name alone is excellent; his glory is above the earth and heaven.*
> Psalm 148:7-13

There are incidents in the Bible where some animals had actual conversations with humans.

The first one we already looked at. It was in the Garden of Eden. A serpent had a conversation with Eve.

I am not a big fan of snakes. Perhaps it has to do with their ancestor and what he did in the garden. I have come close to many snakes, including deadly poisonous ones. If one of them ever started to have a conversation with me, I would be shocked. Why? Very simply put, everyone knows snakes do not talk.

The Fall of Man
By Peter Paul Reubens and Jan Brueghel, the Elder, 1615

It is interesting to note Eve was not shocked at all that the snake spoke to her. Isn't that strange? Maybe not. Perhaps all animals could talk back then.

In another chapter we will see how the prophet Isaiah and then the Apostle John saw some extraterrestrial beings, with strong animals characteristics, which spoke.

There was another interesting incident in the Bible where an animal spoke. As the Children of Israel were heading to their Promised Land, a ruler by the name of Barak from Moab, one of Israel's enemies, was concerned. He hired a prophet, named Balaam, to curse Israel. God told Balaam not to go help Balak. Balaam disobeyed. He saddled his ass and went anyway. On the way to Balak, Balaam and his ass had an encounter with an angel.

And Balaam rose up in the morning, and saddled his ass, and went with the princes of Moab. And God's anger was kindled because he went: and the angel of the LORD stood in the way for an adversary against him. Now he was riding upon his ass, and his two servants were with him. And the ass saw the angel of the LORD standing in the way, and his sword drawn in his hand: and the ass turned aside out of the way, and went into the field: and Balaam smote the ass, to turn her into the way. But the angel of the LORD stood in a path of the vineyards, a wall being on this side, and a wall on that side. And when the ass saw the angel of the LORD, she thrust herself unto the wall, and crushed Balaam's foot against the wall: and he smote her again. And the angel of the LORD went further, and stood in a narrow place, where was no way to turn either to the right hand or to the left. And when the ass saw the angel of the LORD, she fell down under Balaam: and Balaam's anger was kindled, and he smote the ass with a staff.

And the LORD opened the mouth of the ass, and she said unto Balaam, What have I done unto thee, that thou hast smitten me these three times?

And Balaam said unto the ass, Because thou hast mocked me: I would there were a sword in mine hand, for now would I kill thee.

And the ass said unto Balaam, Am not I thine ass, upon which thou hast ridden ever since I was thine unto this day? was I ever wont to do so unto thee? And he said, Nay. Then the LORD opened the eyes of Balaam, and he saw the angel of the LORD standing in the way, and his sword drawn in his hand: and he bowed down his head, and fell flat on the ground.

Then the LORD opened the eyes of Balaam, and he saw the angel of the LORD standing in the way, and his sword drawn in his hand: and he bowed down his head, and fell flat on his face. And the angel of the LORD said unto him, Wherefore hast thou smitten thine ass these three times? behold, I went out to withstand thee, because thy way is perverse before me: And the ass saw me, and turned from me these three times: unless she had turned from me, surely now also I had slain thee, and saved her alive. Numbers 22:-25-33

There are a few interesting things in this passage. From this encounter, and other accounts in the Bible, we learn an angel can be near us but not be visible to us.

In this encounter we seek angels tried to intervene. As Balaam disobeyed God, an angel stood in the way to stop him. Balaam was going to do something he should not do. God sent an angel, carrying a sword, to stop him. Balaam did not see the angel, but his animal did.

I wonder, did God allow his animal to see an angel only during this specific encounter, or can animals see angel's all the time?

Balaam and the Angel
Painting by Gustav Jaeger - 1836

The animal did the smart thing. She went off the path into a field, away from the angel. Balaam responded unkindly by hitting her.

Balaam then continued his journey. They went through a vineyard and came to a place where there was a wall on each side of the path. The angel stood in front of them

74

again. The animal turned aside and went against one of the walls, hurting Balaam's foot. He struck her again.

Balaam then continued on his way. They came to a very narrow place. His animal saw the angel standing in the way again. There was no room to turn aside so she did the next best thing. She stopped and dropped to the ground. Balaam was so angry he hit her with his staff. He had no idea she was saving his life. I wonder how many times an animal tries to protect us, and we misunderstand.

Then, something amazing happened. The animal spoke to Balaam. The Bible does not say the Lord spoke to Balaam *through the ass*. It says, *The Lord opened the mouth of the ass*. She had something she wanted to say, and God made it possible for her to say it in Balaam's own language so he could understand.

Balaam's reaction was interesting. If I were him I would have been completely amazed my animal was talking to me. Instead, he was so angry, he told her he wanted to kill her.

I wonder if his animal did not realize Balaam could not see the angel. Her perception and reaction to the encounter saved his life. I am sure some of you had times when an animal tried to save your life. I wonder if you recognized that and how you responded.

I believe many times animals try to tell us something, but they cannot speak our language and we often do not listen to them, just like we do often do not listen to God or the people He sends our way.

Questions for Thought or Discussion
Chapter 7
Animals Have Something to Say

1. Can animals talk? If so, how do they talk?

2. Why do most people not communicate with animals?

3. What often happens when someone tries to communicate with animals?

4. What does Psalm 148:7-13 tell us about animals?

5. What animal does the Bible say spoke with Eve in the garden? Did she seem alarmed an animal was speaking to her?

6. When an angel tried to stop the prophet Balaam what did his animal do?

7. How did the prophet Balaam's ass speak with him? Did he seem surprised?

Chapter 8

Our God Given Responsibilities To Animals

And God said, Let us make man in our image, after our likeness: and let them have dominion over the fish of the sea, and over the fowl of the air, and over the cattle, and over all the earth, and over every creeping thing that creepeth upon the earth. Genesis 1:26

Starting way back in the Garden of Eden, right after God created animals and man, He gave man the responsibility to take care of all the creatures He made. God gave man *dominion* over the animals.

When many think of someone having dominion, they think of someone dominating or ruling over someone or something. They often picture the authority a person with dominion holds, but usually forget the administrative responsibility. To have dominion means *to have authority and administrative responsibility.*

God gave man the authority and administrative responsibility to take care of the world and all its creatures. That was a mandate. That mandate extended to taking care of all animals. It even included the *creeping things.*

Many people do not like responsibilities. They like to avoid them and do what they want. Most never consider the fact God says it is our responsibility to take care of all the animals in the world. Have you considered that? What are you doing to fulfill that responsibility?

Some people may say, I am fulfilling that responsibility by taking care of my pets. Others may say, I do not have any animals, so that does not apply to me. Both are wrong. God expects us to take care of our own animals but gave us the

responsibility is to make sure all animals are cared for. Mankind as a whole has neglected that responsibility for a long time.

Adam and Eve in the Garden of Eden
By Johann Wenzel Pieter, 1745-1829

Too many people use and abuse animals. The Bible teaches us you can tell if a person loves God by the way they treat animals.

A righteous man regardeth the life of his beast: but the tender mercies of the wicked are cruel. Proverbs 12:10

Righteous People, ones who seek to live according to God's principles, consciously consider what is best for their animals. Do you do that?

On the other hand, the Bible says those who treat animals cruelly, are Wicked People.

God knows too many rarely consider the proper care of animals, so He included some provisions for their care in the laws He gave to man. He even included a provision to take care of animals in the Ten Commandments.

But the seventh day is the sabbath of the LORD thy God:

in it thou shalt not do any work, thou, nor thy son, nor thy daughter, nor thy manservant, nor thy maidservant, nor thine ox, nor thine ass, nor any of thy cattle, nor thy stranger that is within thy gates; that thy manservant and thy maidservant may rest as well as thou. Deuteronomy 5:14

Most like the idea that commandment says we should take a day of rest. Many leave out the part about honoring God on that day. There is another often overlooked part of that command. God said that day of rest was also for ox, ass, and cattle. That is talking about working animals. Many people violate that command and do not give working animals a day of rest.

There are some who try to follow that principle and do not use their work animals one day a week. Others argue it is not possible to apply that principle with some animals, such as dairy cows.

My wife grew up on a farm. Her father raised dairy cows. Those cows were milked two times a day, every day. Some farmers milk their cows three times a day. They say if you do not milk them at least twice a day, the cows can get a disease called *mastitis*, or they will also stop giving milk. Neither is an option most farmers want.

How do you deal with the commandment which says even cattle are to get a day of rest?. Many respond saying that is an Old Testament Law and we are no longer under the Law so that does not apply anymore. Do you dismiss the other commandments? Is it okay to kill, commit adultery, and covet?

Keeping the Ten Commandments never saved anyone. They were given to provide principles for our personal protection. They help individuals and societies live lives which honor God and each other.

The purpose of a Sabbath Day, was to help us designate a day of rest and a day to worship God. That is a good thing. God designed us to need a day of rest. Without that command, many people would work every day, or make others work every day. Animals need that day of rest too.

The Old Testament Sabbath Day was Saturday, the seventh day of the week. The Jewish day starts at sundown. When the sun sets on Friday the seventh day, Saturday, the Sabbath Day begins.

Orthodox Jews and Seventh-Day Adventists are two groups which believe in keeping the Old Testament Sabbath. Back in the 1960's the Agriculture Department at *Ambassador College*, a Seventh-Day Adventist school in the United Kingdom, discovered age-old way to provide cows a Sabbath Day rest.

They learned that many years ago cows were milked only once a day. The milking took place in the morning. After they were milked, the cows were put with their calves during the day. The calves feed directly on their mother's milk. At night the calves were separated from their mothers. By the next morning the cows were full and were milked again.

That procedure was followed every day except Friday. On Friday, when the sun went down and the Sabbath began, the calves were kept with the mothers overnight. The cows were not milked on Saturday. The calves stayed with their mothers until Saturday evening, when they were separated. On Sunday morning, they started milking the cows again.

That procedure did not produce as much milk, as it does when you milk cows two or three times a day, but it showed you could honor the sabbath day principle. It also produced healthier cows and calves.

I am not saying that is how you must conduct a dairy business. I am saying, if a person believes they should give their cows a day of rest there is a way to do that.

The important thing is God wants us to treat all animals kindly, including working animals.

God included another provision in the law to protect and provide for animals.

Thou shalt not muzzle the ox when he treadeth out the corn.   Deuteronomy 25:4

Years ago, some animals were put to work extracting grain from sheaves. One method had the oxen walk around a pile of grain. Their continued walking over the sheaves helped extract the grain. Another method hitched the oxen to a beam connected to a grinding stone.

While those animals worked it was not unusual for them to bend over and eat some grain. Some people did not want the animals eating their grain, so they muzzled them to stop them from eating. God put a provision in the law prohibiting the muzzling of work animals.

Treading Out the Corn
Engraving by C. Coursen, Picture by R, Beavis, 1885

The word *corn*, used in that passage, is an old English word which meant grain. When the King James Version of the Bible was translated, the word *corn* did not mean what we mean when we use the word today. It meant grain. That included wheat, oats, barley, and rye.

When Europeans came to the Americas they were introduced to a new grain, unlike any other they knew. It grew on stalks, like most grains, but with many grains on long cobs. They called it *corn* because it was a grain. Today, the word *corn* almost universally is reserved for that corn, native to the Americas, which grows on a cob.

Some countries take the responsibility of taking care of animals very seriously. Some have Departments of Agriculture, Commerce and Conservation. They protect wildlife and natural resources. Some do much good.

Some societies, such as the *Audubon Society*, were formed to help try to stop the extinction of some species.

Some organizations seek to protect animals from abuse and neglect, such as the *American Society for the Prevention of Cruelty of Animals* (ASPCA) and the *North Shore Animal League*.

Some view raising animals for food as being cruel to animals. After the world-wide flood God said both man and beast could eat meat. Since that time, some animals are raised to eat. God expects us to take good care of them. When they are killed for food it should be done in a way which causes them the least amount of pain.

Some view hunting as cruel. In some cases it is cruel. It is okay to hunt for food but hunting as a sport, or hunting solely for trophies, seems especially cruel.

> *The slothful man roasteth not that which he took in hunting: but the substance of a diligent man is precious.*
> Proverbs 12:27

It is important to do what we can do to take care of animals. It is sad some people place the protection of animal life over human life. It is ironic some fight to save the whales but do nothing to stop the murder of unborn human babies.

Questions for Thought or Discussion
Chapter 8
Our God Given Responsibility to Animals

1. What responsibility did God give Adam and Eve regarding animals?

2. How has man done with that responsibility?

3. Contrast how a Wicked Person and a Righteous Person treat animals.

4. Which of the Ten Commandments gives man a responsibility regarding animals? What is that responsibility?

5. What animals does the Bible exempt from that commandment?

6. How were people told to treat working animals who worked with grain?

7. Are eating animals or hunting cruel?

Chapter 9

Strange Extraterrestrial Beings

As we consider what the Bible says about animals and the question, *where do animals go when they die,* there are some other interesting observations worth noting. In this chapter we are going to look at descriptions in the Bible of some strange extraterrestrial beings. This may seem bizarre and unrelated to the question, *where do animals go when they die,* until you discover the descriptions of those beings describe all of them as having some animal characteristics.

Over the years some people claimed they had encounters with extraterrestrial beings. Some are clearly hoaxes, but are they all? Most describe seeing unusual beings unlike anything living on Earth.

Some popular science-fiction movies, like *Star Wars,* introduced extraterrestrials with characteristics similar to some animals on Earth.

You may be surprised to learn the Bible gives detailed descriptions of some extraterrestrial beings. It is important to understand the word *extraterrestrial* means *something not from this world.* According to that definition, in one sense God himself is an extraterrestrial being because He is not from this world. God is actually *superterrestrial,* above this world or anything in the universe, as He is the creator.

It is important you understand my perspective on this, otherwise the rest of what I say will not make sense. I believe the Biblical account of creation. I believe God created the world and made all life in one week. I also believe He spoke with man right away. That may sound silly to some, especially those who do not know there is more scientific proof for creation by an intelligent designer, than there is for evolution. It is not my purpose to try to prove that, but you must understand where I am coming from to understand my conclusions.

Most evolutionists teach man created the concept of God. They say man needed some way to answer things they did not understand, so they came up with the idea of God. They say people defined God according their own ideas and gave God certain human characteristics. That is called *anthropomorphism.*

I disagree with evolutionists. I accept the Biblical account of creation and let God define himself. The Bible teaches God not only created man but spoke with him. That means our original base of knowledge, our vocabulary and our first language came directly from God. God spoke with man. He gave man words to describe Himself and the world He made.

Many times we do not fully understand the significance or true meaning of some words God gave us. For example, consider the following verse.

> *He shall cover thee with His feathers, and under His wings shalt thou trust: His truth shall be thy shield and buckler.* Psalm 91:3

Most people picture God looking like us. After all, the Bible says we were created *in the image of God.* Yet, Psalm 91:3 says God has wings with feathers. Humans obviously do not have wings.

The evolutionist say, in this passage, man ascribed that animal characteristic to God. But as a creationist I take the Bible literally. If it says God has wings, then God has wings.

We must keep in mind God gave man the word *wing* to describe something He has. It might be similar to what birds have, but is not exactly the same.

Some say this is poetical or symbolic language. It is true the Bible does contain some poetical or symbolic language. Such poetical or symbolic language make it clear it is symbolic by using words such as *like* or *as*, when drawing symbolic comparisons. This passage does not make that distinction.

Some will say the statement, *His truth shall be thy shield and buckler* is clearly symbolic. But is it? God's truth is not only symbolically a shield, but His truth also literally shields us from error.

Though that verse says God has wings, one day God and three angels visited Abraham. When they did, it does not appear Abraham saw wings on any of them. He mistook them for humans.

> *And the LORD appeared unto him in the plains of Mamre: and he sat in the tent door in the heat of the day; And he lift up his eyes and looked, and, lo, three men stood by him: and when he saw them, he ran to meet them from the tent door, and bowed himself toward the ground.* Genesis 18:1-3

Though some extraterrestrial beings described in the Bible look like humans, some have predominant animal characteristics and could never be mistaken for humans.

One day the prophet Ezekiel had an encounter with an unidentified flying object and some unusual extraterrestrial beings. He gave a very detailed description of his encounter.

> *And I looked, and, behold, a whirlwind came out of the north, a great cloud, and a fire infolding itself, and a brightness was about it, and out of the midst thereof as the colour of amber, out of the midst of the fire. Also out of the midst thereof came the likeness of four living creatures. And this was their appearance; they had the likeness of a man. And every one had four faces, and every one had four wings. And their feet were straight feet; and the sole of their feet was like the sole of a calf's foot: and they sparkled like the colour of burnished brass. And they had the hands of a man under their wings on their four sides; and they four had their faces and their wings. Their wings were joined one to another; they turned not when they went; they went every one straight forward. As for the likeness of their faces, they four had the face of a man, and the face of a lion, on the right side: and they four had the face of an*

ox on the left side; they four also had the face of an eagle. Thus were their faces: and their wings were stretched upward; two wings of every one were joined one to another, and two covered their bodies. And they went every one straight forward: whither the spirit was to go, they went; and they turned not when they went. As for the likeness of the living creatures, their appearance was like burning coals of fire, and like the appearance of lamps: it went up and down among the living creatures; and the fire was bright, and out of the fire went forth lightning. And the living creatures ran and returned as the appearance of a flash of lightning.

Now as I beheld the living creatures, behold one wheel upon the earth by the living creatures, with his four faces. The appearance of the wheels and their work was like unto the colour of a beryl: and they four had one likeness: and their appearance and their work was as it were a wheel in the middle of a wheel. When they went, they went upon their four sides: and they turned not when they went. As for their rings, they were so high that they were dreadful; and their rings were full of eyes round about them four.

And when the living creatures went, the wheels went by them: and when the living creatures were lifted up from the earth, the wheels were lifted up. Whithersoever the spirit was to go, they went, thither was their spirit to go; and the wheels were lifted up over against them: for the spirit of the living creature was in the wheels. When those went, these went; and when those stood, these stood; and when those were lifted up from the earth, the wheels were lifted up over against them: for the spirit of the living creature was in the wheels. And the likeness of the firmament upon the heads of the living creature was as the colour of the terrible crystal, stretched forth over their heads above. And under the firmament were their wings straight, the one toward the other: every one had two, which covered on this side, and every one had two, which covered on that side, their bodies. And when they went, I heard the noise of their wings, like the noise of great waters, as the voice of the Almighty, the voice of speech, as the noise of an host: when they stood, they let down their wings. And there was a voice from the

firmament that was over their heads, when they stood, and had let down their wings.
And above the firmament that was over their heads was the likeness of a throne, as the appearance of a sapphire stone: and upon the likeness of the throne was the likeness as the appearance of a man above upon it.

Ezekiel 1:4-26

Ezekiel's Vision
Engraving by Bernard Pickart (1693-1783)

When Ezekiel wrote that passage he was not writing symbolically. He gave a detailed literal description of what he saw. His encounter started with a whirlwind, a folding of clouds, and some fire and lightening. Then he saw four very unusual beings. They each had a mix of human and animal characteristics. He also saw a spherical flying object, and someone sitting on a throne high above them who spoke to him.

The arrival and appearance of the flying object sounds similar to some portrayals of spaceships. He described what he saw as looking like a wheel moving within a wheel. It had many lights, which looked like eyes.

Similar sightings were reported more than two thousand years later. I am not saying those people saw what Ezekiel saw but maybe they did.

The beings Ezekiel described were unlike anything on earth. They defied normal physical laws. They levitated, flew, moved as fast as lightening, and glowed like fire.

Ezekiel said the beings looked similar to men but had animal characteristics. They had hands and legs like a man, but their feet were like a calf's foot. They each had four wings. Each had four faces: one face looked like a man, one like a lion, one like an ox, and the other like an eagle.

Later in the *Book of Ezekiel*, he wrote about another encounter with the same beings in the temple in Jerusalem. That time he described one of their faces as the face of a cherub, instead of saying the face of a human. That lets us know humans and cherubs have similar faces.

> *And the cherubims were lifted up. This is the living creature that I saw by the river of Chebar.*
>
> Ezekiel 10:15

In the second encounter, Ezekiel identified the beings he previously saw as *cherubim*. Most artistic representations of cherubs show them as fat baby angels. That is quite different from Ezekiel's description.

Are cherubs, a type of angel? I believe they are.

Look at what the Bible says about Lucifer. He was an angel who lead a rebellion against God. He is now called Satan and the Devil.

> *Thou art the anointed cherub that covereth; and I have set thee so: thou wast upon the holy mountain of God;*

*thou hast walked up and down in the midst of the stones
of fire.*   Ezekiel 28:14

Satan is called an *anointed cherub*. The fact Satan is an
angel, and also called a cherub, means a cherub is a type of
angel.

*And the cherubims shall stretch forth their wings on
high, covering the mercy seat with their wings, and
their faces shall look one to another; toward the mercy
seat shall the faces of the cherubims be.*
                                     Exodus 25:20

God instructed Moses to build the *Ark of the Covenant*
and put two cherubs with wings on top of the ark. The fact
those cherubs had wings, and cherubs are a type of angel,
lets us know some angels have wings.

The Historical drawings of the Ark of the Covenant make
the cherubs on the ark appear humanlike with two wings.

Ark of the Covenant
Uncredited Engraving from Holy Bible, 1883

When God expelled Adam and Eve from the Garden of
Eden He placed cherubim outside the garden with a
flaming sword. No description is given of what they looked
like. I wonder if they looked like the two cherubs over the

ark, or like the ones Ezekiel saw? I am sure they did not look like fat baby angels.

> So he drove out the man; and he placed at the east of the garden of Eden Cherubims, and a flaming sword which turned every way, to keep the way of the tree of life.
>
> Genesis 3:24

Most of us picture angels looking similar to humans, yet with wings, which most of us consider an animal characteristic.

In some encounters in the Bible angels are mistaken for humans. The beings Ezekiel encountered had wings but did not look human.

Some accounts describe angels as flying. People therefore assume all angels have wings. It must be noted, there is not one instance in the Bible where a being people personally encountered, which were specifically called an *angel*, is described as having wings. If cherubs are a type of angel, then some angels have wings but that does not mean all angels do.

Historically, the earliest artistic image of an angel ever discovered is from the 3rd Century. It is in the *Catacomb of Priscilla* and depicts an angel without wings.

The earliest known image of an angel with wings was discovered near Istanbul in Turkey. It is from 379-395 A.D., in the 4th Century. It is on the *Prince's Sarcophagus*. After that time angels appear in many illustrations with wings.

Some use a passage from Zechariah to try to prove angels have wings.

> Then the angel that talked with me went forth, and said unto me, Lift up now thine eyes, and see what is this that goeth forth. And I said, What is it? And he said, This is an ephah that goeth forth. He said moreover, This is their resemblance through all the earth. And, behold, there was lifted up a talent of lead: and this is a woman that sitteth in the midst of the ephah. And he said, This is wickedness. And he cast it into the midst of the ephah; and he cast the weight of lead upon the mouth thereof. Then lifted I up mine eyes, and looked, and, behold, there

came out two women, and the wind was in their wings;
for they had wings like the wings of a stork: and they
lifted up the ephah between the earth and the heaven.
Zechariah 5:5-9

Most Bible scholars understand this to be a prophesy about God's people. An angel talks with Zechariah. The angel is not described. God's people are pictured as a women in a basket (ephah), with a heavy lid, being carried far away into long-term captivity by two women with stork-like wings. It does not say the women are angels.

I never met a woman with wings. Wings are not a human characteristic. He described those women as having storks wings. Storks have big strong wings. Storks were listed in the Bible as an unclean bird. They were usually considered a symbol of evil.

Those two flying women were carrying God's people into captivity. What were those flying winged-women? Zechariah did not call them angels, but they were clearly extraterrestrial beings. Could they have been demons, which are fallen angels? The Bible does not say.

Isaiah, another Old Testament prophet, saw a different group of extraterrestrial beings. He called them *seraphim*. Seraphim means *burning ones*. He saw them around God's throne. He does not say anything about their appearance except each had six wings. Some assume they were angels.

In the year that king Uzziah died I saw also the Lord
sitting upon a throne, high and lifted up, and his train
filled the temple. Above it stood the seraphims: each one
had six wings; with twain he covered his face, and with
twain he covered his feet, and with twain he did fly. And
one cried unto another, and said, Holy, holy, holy, is the
LORD of hosts: the whole earth is full of His glory.
Isaiah 6:1-5

It is interesting to note, Isaiah said the seraphim spoke words which praised God.

Many years later, it appears John the Apostle saw the same beings as Isaiah. In the *Book of Revelation,* he said he saw beings with six wings around the throne of God. He gave more details about those beings.

> *And before the throne there was a sea of glass like unto crystal: and in the midst of the throne, and round about the throne, were four beasts full of eyes before and behind. And the first beast was like a lion, and the second beast like a calf, and the third beast had a face as a man, and the fourth beast was like a flying eagle.*
>
> Revelation 4:6-7

Unlike the four beings in Ezekiel, which looked alike, these four were different from each other. Each only had one face. Each had one of the four faces Ezekiel saw.

Isaiah called the beings *seraphim*. In Revelation they were called *beasts*. That is the translation of the Greek word, *zoon*, which means *living creature*, or *animal*.

Each of those beings had six wings. Each were described as looking *like* something. The first looked *like* a lion. It did not say it *was* a lion. Whatever it was, it was similar to a lion. The second looked like a calf. The third had a face like a man. The fourth looked like a flying eagle.

The Apostle John's Vision of Heaven
The Four Seraphim are around God on the Throne
By Matthias Gerung in the Uttheinrich Bible, 1530-1532

And the four beasts had each of them six wings about him; and they were full of eyes within: and they rest not day and night, saying, Holy, holy, holy, Lord God Almighty, which was, and is, and is to come. And when those beasts give glory and honour and thanks to him that sat on the throne, who liveth for ever. The four and twenty elders fall down before him that sat on the throne, and worship him that liveth for ever and ever, and cast their crowns before the throne, saying, Thou art worthy, O Lord, to receive glory and honour and power: for thou hast created all things, and for thy pleasure they are and were created.   Revelation 4:8-11

Just as in Isaiah, those four beings spoke. Though three of them had animal heads, they did not make animal sounds, they spoke understandable words. The words they spoke gave glory to God and acknowledged Him as their Creator.

And all the angels stood round about the throne, and about the elders and the four beasts, and fell before the throne on their faces, and worshipped God.
                                    Revelation 7:11

Some speculate seraphim, like the cherubim, are a type of angel. However, this passage differentiates between the angels and the seraphim. It says all the angels, *and* the four beasts, the seraphim, stood before God. It lists them separately. It appears seraphim are not angels.

In Ezekiel, Zechariah, Isaiah, and Revelation, we saw three unique encounters with extraterrestrial beings. In both encounters the beings all had animal characteristics

It is important to remember God created everything. It should not be a surprise some things on earth may look similar to things in Heaven. It appears God created animals on earth, which look like some extraterrestrial animal-like creatures which He made in Heaven.

In all the above encounters the extraterrestrial beings looked similar to something on earth, yet different.

There are other passages in scripture where extraterrestrial beings look just like beings seen on earth. Many are referred to by the same names as their earthly counter-parts. It appears God made some animals on earth to look like some in Heaven.

One of the most common extraterrestrial beings sighted is a horse. Look at the following passages.

> *I saw by night, and behold a man riding upon a red horse, and he stood among the myrtle trees that were in the bottom; and behind him were there red horses, speckled, and white. Then said I, O my lord, what are these? And the angel that talked with me said unto me, I will shew thee what these be. And the man that stood among the myrtle trees answered and said, These are they whom the LORD hath sent to walk to and fro throughout the earth.* Zechariah 1:8-10

In this passage, Zechariah, who saw the four seraphim, was talking with a man whom he later said was an angel. While they were talking, there appeared a man on a red horse who had three other horses with him. The rider and horses were not earthly beings. They appear to be supernatural. Supernatural means *something which operates above the laws of nature.*

In the B*ook of Revelation* a red horse is seen, along with three other horses. Perhaps they are the same ones seen in Zechariah.

> *And I saw when the Lamb opened one of the seals, and I heard, as it were the noise of thunder, one of the four beasts saying, Come and see. And I saw, and behold a white horse: and he that sat on him had a bow; and a crown was given unto him: and he went forth conquering, and to conquer. And when he had opened the second seal, I heard the second beast say, Come and see. And there went out another horse that was red: and power was given to him that sat thereon to take peace from the earth, and that they should kill one another: and there was given unto him a great sword. And when he had opened the third seal, I heard the third beast say, Come and see. And I beheld, and lo a black horse; and he that sat on him had a pair of balances in his hand. And I heard a voice in the midst of the four beasts say, A measure of wheat for a penny, and three measures of*

barley for a penny; and see thou hurt not the oil and the wine. And when he had opened the fourth seal, I heard the voice of the fourth beast say, Come and see. And I looked, and behold a pale horse: and his name that sat on him was Death, and Hell followed with him. And power was given unto them over the fourth part of the earth, to kill with sword, and with hunger, and with death, and with the beasts of the earth.

Revelation 6:1-8

Four Horsemen of the Apocalypse
By Peter Von Cornelius, 1845

Revelation 6:1-8 speaks of what is commonly called *The Four Horsemen of the Apocalypse.* It does not say they rode something *like* horses. It says what they rode *were* horses. It appears horses on earth were made to look just like extraterrestrial supernatural horses.

And I saw heaven opened, and behold a white horse; and he that sat upon him was called Faithful and True, and in righteousness he doth judge and make war. His eyes were as a flame of fire, and on his head were many crowns; and he had a name written, that no man knew, but he himself. And he was clothed with a vesture dipped

in blood: and his name is called The Word of God. And the armies which were in heaven followed him upon white horses, clothed in fine linen, white and clean.
Revelation 19:11-14

Revelation 19 say Jesus Christ will come down from Heaven, to Earth, riding a white horse. He is followed by armies from Heaven, all riding white horses. Are those horses heavenly horses or resurrected ones? We will have to wait until that day to find the answer to that question

That event is prophetic. It takes place after the resurrection of the dead in Christ. I am excited, as a follower of Jesus Christ, to know I will be one of those coming back on a white horse. Will you be one?

Jesus does not need to come back on a horse, yet He does. The Bible says all the animals on earth look forward to His return. I believe He shows how much He loves animals when He chooses to include horses as part of His triumphant second coming.

Questions for Thought or Discussion
Chapter 9
Strange Extraterrestrial Beings

1. What does *extraterrestrial* mean?

2. What does the Bible mean when it says God has wings, which are an animal characteristic?

3. Describe Elijah's unique encounter with some extraterrestrials and a unique vehicle. What animal characteristics were mentioned?

4. What name did Elijah ascribe to the beings he encountered.

5. Do all angels have wings?

6. Isaiah and John the Apostle describe seraphim. What animal characteristics do they have?

7. What is one of the most common extraterrestrial beings mentioned in the Bible which looks like an animal on earth?

Chapter 10

Unusual Animals & Dinosaurs

This chapter takes a look at some unusual animals mentioned in the Bible. That includes dragons, unicorns, Behemoth, Leviathan, and a great fish that swallowed a man. This chapter also attempts to answer the question, how do dinosaurs fit with the Bible?

Dragons and unicorn are considered mythical beings by many, yet the Bible refers to them numerous times as actual animals. We will take a look at them in this chapter.

The Bible tells the story of how a man was swallowed by a great fish and came out alive after three days and three nights. Some consider that a myth, yet Christ referred to that as an actual event.

Two of these unusual creatures, mentioned in the Bible, Behemoth and Leviathan, may have been dinosaurs.

In the Bible there are many symbolic images of unusual animals used to prophetically represent people or powers. This chapter does not look at the symbolic beings but at the actual unusual real animals mentioned in the Bible.

Dragons

What comes to your mind when you hear the word *dragon*? Many picture a large, powerful, serpent-like creature.

Dragons have been part of stories all over the world for thousands of years. They appear in ancient legends and in various drawings. Many consider them mythical beings.

It should be noted, many scholars agree myths are usually based on some kind of fact. Some myths are based on historical events or people. They are often called myths because they are hard to believe.

It is interesting how different cultures, far removed from one another, have stories of dragons. It appears people around the world had encounters with animals which can be called dragons. Many of those stories are called myths.

Dragons are often portrayed by Europeans as large fierce serpent-like winged, evil creatures.

In Chinese lore they are similar but different. They are pictured as serpent-like creatures, yet without wings. Unlike the Europeans, the Chinese stories portray dragons as benevolent creatures.

The ancient Babylonians worshiped a god named *Marduk* (also called *Bel)* as far back as 1119 B.C. His companion was a dragon named *Mushussu*. Mushussu was a winged, serpent creature with scales. He had some characteristics of a fish, an eagle, and a lion.

The stories of *Marduk* and *Mushussu* continued for five hundred years into the Persian reign of Cyrus the Great (c. 590-525 B.C.).

During Medieval Times (5th through 15th Century A.D.) there are stories of medieval knights fighting dragons.

Saint George Killing the Dragon
Likhauri, Ozurget, Georgia, 12th Century

In 1260, there was a story called *The Golden Legend*. It tells how Saint George, in the late 3rd Century A.D., fought a winged serpentine dragon, near Libya. The dragon lived in a pond and terrorized the area. Every year the people selected one young person to offer to the dragon to appease it. One year the lot fell on the king's daughter. Saint George rescued the princess and later killed the dragon. Saint George later became the Patron Saint of England.

The belief in dragons was so strong in some cultures that some countries adopted dragons on their flags or crests. A red dragon became the symbol of the Country of Wales and of Scotland. A white dragon became the symbol of England. The country of Bhutan, in Asia, also use a dragon as their symbol.

Image of a Dragon from Medieval Manuscript
MS Harley, 1260 A.D.

Many depictions of dragons in modern lore resemble an image found in a Medieval manuscript from 1260 called *MS*

Harley. It depicts a long fire-breathing, serpent-like creature with a ridged back, horns, and wings.

Dragons are mentioned in both the Old and New Testament. The word *dragon* appears in eight different books of the Bible.

In the Old Testament, the Hebrew word *tanniyim* is translated twenty-eight times as *dragon(s).* It means a non-mythical elongated serpent-like creature. It is translated three times as *serpent,* three times as *whale(s),* and one time as *sea monster.* In modern translations it is sometimes translated as *dinosaur.*

Serpent does not appear to be a good translation of *tanniyim.* The Bible often differentiates between dragons and serpents. When the word *serpent (nachash)* is used in the Bible, after Genesis chapter three, it refers to legless, slithering creatures we usually call *snakes.* Though dragons are defined as serpent-like, they are different creatures.

Some verses describe some characteristics of dragons.

Their wine is the poison of dragons, and the cruel venom of asps. Deuteronomy 32:33

In the Book of Deuteronomy, dragons are mentioned as having poisonous venom.

I am a brother to dragons, and a companion to owls. Job 30:29

Owls and dragons are mentioned together a few times. Owls are mainly an animal which is active at night. Are the dragons being referred to in the Bible basically creatures of the night?

Nebuchadrezzar the king of Babylon hath devoured me, he hath crushed me, he hath made me an empty vessel, he hath swallowed me up like a dragon, he hath filled his belly with my delicates, he hath cast me out.
Jeremiah 51:34

The prophet Jeremiah referred to the dragon's ability to devour a human. They must have been enormously large creatures. That description agrees with the later medieval descriptions of dragons eating people.

There are a few times dragons are used symbolically in the Bible to help people picture a truth. Pharaoh of Egypt is called a great dragon and described as lying in a river like a real dragon. Apparently some dragons were huge and like to lay in rivers.

> *Speak, and say, Thus saith the Lord GOD; Behold, I am against thee, Pharaoh king of Egypt, the great dragon that lieth in the midst of his rivers, which hath said, My river is mine own, and I have made it for myself.*
>
> Ezekiel 29:3

In the New Testament, the Greek word *drakon* is translated *dragon*. It describes the same creature as the *tanniyim* in the Old Testament. It means a large serpent-like creature.

> *And there appeared another wonder in heaven; and behold a great red dragon, having seven heads and ten horns, and seven crowns upon his heads. And his tail drew the third part of the stars of heaven, and did cast them to the earth: and the dragon stood before the woman which was ready to be delivered, for to devour her child as soon as it was born.* Revelation 12:3-4

The Book of Revelation used the image of a dragon, ready to eat a child, to represent Satan. It described his fall from heaven, his persecution of the church, and his political influence.

> *And he laid hold on the dragon, that old serpent, which is the Devil, and Satan, and bound him a thousand years.* Revelation 20:2

Later in the Book of Revelation Satan is called the dragon and that old serpent. No wonder people familiar with the Bible considered dragons evil.

We must be careful we do not call all dragons evil just because Satan is symbolically referred to as a dragon. Satan is also referred to as a lion in 1 Peter 5:8.

> *Be sober, be vigilant; because your adversary the devil,*

*as a roaring lion, walketh about, seeking whom he may
devour.* 1 Peter 5:8

The family of Judah in the Book of Genesis is referred to
as a lion. That symbolism carried down to Jesus of
Nazareth, one of the descendants of Judah.

*Judah is a lion's whelp: from the prey, my son, thou art
gone up: he stooped down, he couched as a lion, and as
an old lion; who shall rouse him up?* Genesis 49:9

It is clear from history, and the Bible, people had
encounters with huge serpent-like creatures called
dragons. There is a possibility dragons were a type of
dinosaur which lived for many years following the world-
wide flood. It is most likely they are now extinct.

Jonah and the Great Fish

*So they took up Jonah, and cast him forth into the sea:
and the sea ceased from her raging. Then the men feared
the LORD exceedingly, and offered a sacrifice unto the
LORD and made vows. Now the LORD had prepared a
great fish to swallow up Jonah. And Jonah was in the
belly of the fish three days and three nights. Then Jonah
prayed unto the LORD his God out of the fish's belly ...
And the LORD spake unto the fish, and it vomited out
Jonah.* Jonah 1:15-2:1, 10

The book of Jonah tells the story of how God told the
prophet Jonah to take his message to the Ninevites. Jonah
ran away from God rather than taking God's message to the
Ninevites. They were a cruel people, which oppressed
Jonah's people. Jonah did not want God to forgive them.

While Jonah was running away from God, a storm
threatened to sink the ship he was in. Jonah admitted to
the others he was running away from God and was the
cause of the storm. Instead of praying for forgiveness and
doing what God commanded, Jonah wanted to die. He told

the sailors to throw him overboard. They tried to save his life then reluctantly threw him overboard.

Instead of letting Jonah die. God sent a *great fish* to swallow him. It took three days in that fish for Jonah to pray. When Jonah was finally willing to take God's message to the people Jonah wanted punished, God had the great fish vomit him out. Jonah must have been a scarry sight after three days in the digestive juices in the fish's belly.

Jonah and the Great Fish
Oil Painting by Pieter Lashman, 1621

Some children's version of the story of Jonah say he was swallowed by a whale. In the Bible, the Hebrew *dawg*, is used to describe the creature which swallowed Jonah. That word is translated as *fish* all twenty times it is used in the Old Testament.

A different Hebrew word is translated as *whale* in the Old Testament. It is the word *tanniym*, the same word translated as *dragon* or dinosaur. That is not the word used to describe what swallowed Jonah. He was swallowed by some type of extremely large fish.

There are some fish large enough to swallow a man, but

none known in which a man can live for three days.

There was obviously miraculous intervention by God on behalf of Jonah. The Bible says *God prepared* that fish for Jonah. Did God have it grow extra-large, or did he have it develop a digestive system which would allow Jonah to live? What we do know is, that fish obeyed God and swallowed Jonah and later obeyed God and spit him out.

Some say the story of Jonah is a myth. Jesus mentioned Jonah as an historical person and used Jonah being swallowed by a great fish as an illustration of his death and resurrection.

Do such fish, as swallowed Jonah, exist today?

Unicorns

DE MONOCEROTE.

Figura hæc talis est, qualis à pictoribus ferè hodie pingitur, de qua certi nihil habeo.

Woodcut Illustration of a Unicorn
Historiae Animalium, Vol. 1. Conrad Gessner, 1551

What comes to your mind when you hear the word unicorn? Do you picture a wild ox or a rhinoceros? Some people claim that is what is meant by the word unicorn.

When most people picture a unicorn they picture a horse with a long horn in the middle of its head. Many believe unicorns are a mythical animal. That was not always the case.

An image of a unicorn as a horse-like creature, with a horn in the middle of its head, is found in a scientific encyclopedia. In 1551, Conrad Gessner, a physician and well-respected professor published the first of his five volume illustrated work entitled, *Historiae Animalium,* in Zurich. It was an encyclopedia of all know animals from his time. It included narratives from ancient naturalists, including Aristotle and Pliny. The first volume, published in 1551, was titled *Live Bearing Four-footed Animals.* That volume included the *De Monocerote* (unicorn).

The word *unicorn* appears in five different books in the Bible.

> *God brought them out of Egypt; he hath as it were the strength of an unicorn.*   Numbers 23:22

> *God brought him forth out of Egypt; he hath as it were the strength of an unicorn: he shall eat up the nations his enemies, and shall break their bones, and pierce them through with his arrows.*   Numbers 24:8

The Book of Numbers refers to the strength of the unicorn. Oxen and rhinoceros are both strong like that.

> *Will the unicorn be willing to serve thee, or abide by thy crib? Canst thou bind the unicorn with his band in the furrow? or will he harrow the valleys after thee?*
>   Job 39:9-10

The Book of Job compares the unicorn to a work horse, but says it cannot be tamed or used as a work animal. Oxen can be tamed so that rules out unicorns being oxen. Animals trainers claim Rhinoceros can be trained, though it is difficult.

> *He maketh them also to skip like a calf; Lebanon and Sirion like a young unicorn.*   Psalm 29:6

Psalm 29:6 refers to unicorns as skipping like a calf. That clearly rules out both oxen and rhinoceroses.

There is a good possibility the description of a unicorn as a horse-like creature is correct. Gessner claims such a creature lived in his day. If the unicorn is as Gessner described, it like many other animals, is most likely extinct.

Dinosaurs and the Bible

The word *dinosaur* does not appear in the Bible. Some people think that is a problem. How can a book which tells us how the world was created and how man came to exist not mention the word dinosaur?

It must be noted the word *dinosaur* is a relatively new word. It was not used until 1841, when Sir Richard Owen put together two Greek words, *deinos*, which means terrible and *sauros*, which means lizard. Owens used the word *dinosaur* to describe the fossils of large lizards.

The Bible does not specifically mention mice, cats, or woodchucks, yet no one thinks that is a problem. Though the word *dinosaur* does not appear in the Bible, creatures, which appear to be dinosaurs are found in the Bible.

All things were made by him; and without him was not any thing made that was made.　　　　John 1:3

The Bible says God created all things. The Book of Genesis gives a detailed account of that creation. It tells how God made the heavens and the earth. It also says how God created plants, trees, birds, and all animals which live in the sea and on the land. It says He did all that in six days. The fossil record shows dinosaurs lived on the land and in the sea, therefore can God created them.

The fossil record shows us there were many different types of dinosaurs which lived all over the world.

According to scientists who believe in evolution, dinosaurs became extinct before man appeared. They say that could explain why they believe they are not mentioned in the Bible. They say the Bible was written many years before dinosaur fossils were discovered, therefore the writers had no idea dinosaurs existed before them and would not mention something they had no idea existed.

The Bible claims it is written by God and gives an account of how the world was created. It says the world, as well as all animals and man, were created in six literal twenty-four hour days, not over billions of years as some evolutionists claim. That includes all creatures both living and extinct. That includes dinosaurs.

The Bible includes some descriptions of some creatures which appear to be dinosaurs.

On the third day of creation the Authorized King James Bible says God created *great whales*.

> *And God created great whales, and every living creature that moveth, which the waters brought forth abundantly, after their kind, and every winged fowl after his kind: and God saw that it was good.*
>
> Genesis 1:21

The words *great whales* is a translation of the Hebrew words *gadowl* and *tanniym*. The word *gadowl* means great, as in great, large, or mighty. We have seen the word *tanniym* is translated in other places as *dragon, sea monster* or *dinosaur*. Translating *tanniym* as whale does not fit very well with other passages where that word is used. It is very possible that word in Genesis meant dinosaurs or dinosaur-like creatures such as the sea dwelling Plesiosaurus.

Behemoth

> *Behold now behemoth, which I made with thee; he eateth grass as an ox. Lo now, his strength is in his loins, and his force is in the navel of his belly. He moveth his tail like a cedar: the sinews of his stones are wrapped together. His bones are as strong pieces of brass; his bones are like bars of iron. He is the chief of the ways of*

God: he that made him can make his sword to approach unto him. Surely the mountains bring him forth food, where all the beasts of the field play. He lieth under the shady trees, the shady trees cover him with their shadow; the willows of the brook compass him about. Behold, he drinketh up a river, and hasteth not: he trusteth that he can draw up Jordan into his mouth. He taketh it with his eyes: his nose pierceth through snares.
Job 40:15-24

What is a Behemoth? The word Behemoth is only mentioned in the Bible in the Book of Job. Yet, it and Leviathan receive the most detailed descriptions of any animals found in the Bible.

Artist Conception of Behemoth and Leviathan
Engraving by William Blake, 1825

For many years some speculated Behemoth was perhaps an Elephant or Rhinoceros. There are some elements in the description which can apply to both those animals but others which clearly disqualify each of them.

The description mentions his food comes from the mountains. That would work for an Elephant but eliminates the Rhinoceros. The fact his nose pierces through snares would work for the Rhinoceros but eliminates the Elephant. The fact it moves his tail like a cedar implies a long powerful tail. Neither Elephants nor Rhinoceros have long powerful tails.

Brontosaurus
Image from "Extinct Monsters" by H.N. Hutchinson, 1892

The Behemoth is called, *the chief of the ways of God.* That means it is a large, impressive creature. It appears to be extinct. Some scientists believe there is a good possibility Behemoth was a large dinosaur. Some believe it was a *Brontosaurus, Diplodocus* or *Brachiosaurus.*

Leviathan

In that day the LORD with his sore and great and strong sword shall punish leviathan the piercing serpent, even leviathan that crooked serpent; and he shall slay the dragon that is in the sea.   Isaiah 27:1

What is a Leviathan? Leviathans are mentioned in the Bible in the books of Job, Psalms, and Isaiah. A detailed description of Leviathan is given in the Book of Job.

Canst thou draw out leviathan with an hook? or his tongue with a cord which thou lettest down? Canst thou put an hook into his nose? or bore his jaw through with a thorn? Will he make many supplications unto thee? will he speak soft words unto thee? Will he make a covenant with thee? wilt thou take him for a servant for ever? Wilt thou play with him as with a bird? or wilt thou bind him for thy maidens? Shall the companions make a banquet of him? shall they part him among the merchants? Canst thou fill his skin with barbed irons? or his head with fish spears? Lay thine hand upon him, remember the battle, do no more. Behold, the hope of him is in vain: shall not one be cast down even at the sight of him? None is so fierce that dare stir him up: who then is able to stand before me? Who hath prevented me, that I should repay him? whatsoever is under the whole heaven is mine. I will not conceal his parts, nor his power, nor his comely proportion. Who can discover the face of his garment? or who can come to him with his double bridle? Who can open the doors of his face? his teeth are terrible round about. His scales are his pride, shut up together as with a close seal. One is so near to another, that no air can come between them. They are joined one to another, they stick together, that they cannot be sundered. By his neesings a light doth shine, and his eyes are like the eyelids of the morning. Out of his mouth go burning lamps, and sparks of fire leap out. Out of his nostrils goeth smoke, as out of a seething pot or caldron. His breath kindleth coals, and a flame goeth out of his mouth. In his neck remaineth strength, and sorrow is turned into joy before him. The flakes of his flesh are joined together: they are firm in themselves; they cannot be moved. His heart is as firm as a stone; yea, as hard as a piece of the nether millstone. When he raiseth up himself, the mighty are afraid: by reason of breakings they purify themselves. The sword of him that layeth at him cannot hold: the spear, the dart, nor the habergeon. He esteemeth iron as straw, and brass as rotten wood. The arrow cannot make him flee: slingstones are turned with him into stubble. Darts are counted as stubble: he laugheth at the shaking of a spear. Sharp stones are under him: he spreadeth sharp pointed things upon the mire. He maketh the deep to boil like a pot: he maketh the sea like a pot of ointment. He maketh a path to shine after him; one would think the deep to be hoary. Upon earth there is not his like, who is made without fear. He beholdeth all high things: he is a king over all the children of pride. Job 41:1-34

Engraving of a Leviathan from Isaiah 27:1
By Gustave Dore (1832-1883)

We learn a few things about Leviathan from those

passages. It is a large, serpent-like creature found in the sea and rivers. It caused great turbulent movement as it moved around. It had closely fitted, almost impregnable scales. It could not be caught with hooks. Swords and spears had little effect on that creature. It was strong, powerful, and difficult to kill.

A few people believe the Leviathan may be a Crocodile. That seems unlikely as, contrary to the Bible passage, crocodiles are often caught with hooks and spears.

The description of a Leviathan in the Bible does not match any known living creature. It is called a sea monster by some. Some consider it legendary. We know from the Bible it did exist. It may be an extinct dinosaur or more likely a Plesiosaurus type creature.

Depiction of Tiamat from Assyrian Cylinder Seal
8th Century B.C.

The ancient Phoenicians, as far back as 3,000 B.C., had stories of sea monsters which roamed the Great Sea (Mediterranean).

The Assyrians, who were located on the Persian Gulf, believed in a reptilian sea monster called *Tiamat* who fought with the god Bel.

The Persians, another group, believed in a serpent-like sea creature called *Ketus* (Latinized as *Cetus*). It was long with a greyhound type head and split tail.

The Greeks had a story of how the demi-god Hercules killed a Cetus. Could that have been what the Bible refers to as Leviathan? Remember many myths are based on an actual story or historical event.

Persian Ritual Stone of a Sea Nymph Riding a Ketus
Pakistan, 1st Century B.C.

From the Bible and other cultural records, it appears Leviathan was a large fearsome creature which lived in the sea. Some speculate it something like a *Plesiosaurus*. They appear to be extinct, but it is possible some may still live.

Sightings of what has been called the *Loch Ness Monster* in Scotland sound similar to descriptions of Leviathan.

Though the word *dinosaur* does not appear in the Bible, Behemoth and Leviathan and even some dragons mentioned in the Bible are most likely large extinct dinosaurs or Plesiosaurus type creatures. Like all other animals, living and extinct, even a few creatures which some consider mythical, were all created by God.

Questions for Thought or Discussion
Chapter 10
Unusual Animals & Dinosaurs

1. Is it possible some mythological creatures are real?

2. What are some characteristics of dragons in the Bible?

3. What type of creature does the Bible say swallowed the prophet Jonah?

4. What does the Bible say about Unicorns?

5. Why does the word dinosaur not appear in the Bible?

6. How do we know God created dinosaurs?

7. What was a Behemoth?

8. What was a Leviathan?

Chapter 11

The End and a New Beginning

Lift up your eyes to the heavens, and look upon the earth beneath: for the heavens shall vanish away like smoke, and the earth shall wax old like a garment, and they that dwell therein shall die in like manner: but my salvation shall be for ever, and my righteousness shall not be abolished. Isaiah 51:6

But the day of the Lord will come as a thief in the night; in the which the heavens shall pass away with a great noise, and the elements shall melt with fervent heat, the earth also and the works that are therein shall be burned up. 2 Peter 3:10

There is one thing many scientists and the Bible agree on, one day this world as we know it, will come to an end. That is not a doomsday prediction, this is a fact. We are depleting our natural resources and destroying our world.

The Bible says the earth will wear out like an old garment. We can see that happening now. We are polluting our world and wasting our natural resources. We destroyed important habitat and allowed animals to go extinct.

Man has done a poor job fulfilling his responsibility to take care of this world.

To make matter worse, many turn their backs on God. They live for themselves. They chose sin and its fleeting pleasures rather than God and His abundant blessings. They fail to obey God's simple command to love Him and others. As a result, we see painful consequences all around us. Things cannot continue as they are for much longer.

Just as God cleansed the world with a world-wide flood back in Noah's day, He said another cleansing is coming. The moral pollution of our sin and the hurt it causes fills this world and calls for judgment.

For we know that the whole creation groaneth and travaileth in pain together until now. Romans 8:22

Other people, as well as animals, suffer because of our sin. The Bible says they groan within themselves waiting for that day of judgment and their deliverance.

The good news is one day there is going to be an even better new Heaven and a new Earth.

God had the Apostle John write the *Book of Revelation* to tell us what would happen during the earth's final days. That is the time when judgment falls. It is followed by Christ's return to give us a new beginning.

Much of what takes place in the *Book of Revelation* takes place in Heaven. Prior to that book being written, there was no biblical description of what Heaven was like.

Now faith is the substance of things hoped for, the evidence of things not seen. For by it the elders obtained a good report. Through faith we understand that the worlds were framed by the word of God, so that things which are seen were not made of things which do appear. Hebrews 11:1-3

The Book of Hebrews tells of a long parade of faithful individuals, down through time, who choose to follow God, without even having a clear description of Heaven.

Jesus' Disciples followed Him without having any description of Heaven. The night before Jesus died for our sins, which was three years after they chose to follow Him, He made a promise to them.

Let not your heart be troubled: ye believe in God, believe also in me. In my Father's house are many mansions: if it were not so, I would have told you. I go to prepare a place for you. And if I go and prepare a place for you, I will come again, and receive you unto myself; that where I am, there ye may be also. John 14:1-3

Jesus told His disciples He was going to prepare a place for them. He did not describe it in any detail. He just said when it was ready, He would return.

Consider this fact. God made this wonderful world in

just six days. Then consider this, Jesus left to prepare a place for us almost 2,000 years ago. He said, He would return when it was ready. Imagine how beautiful it must be if He has been working on it all that time!

In the *Book of Revelation* we get our first clear glimpse of Heaven.

> *And I beheld, and I heard the voice of many angels round about the throne and the beasts and the elders: and the number of them was ten thousand times ten thousand, and thousands of thousands; Saying with a loud voice, Worthy is the Lamb that was slain to receive power, and riches, and wisdom, and strength, and honour, and glory, and blessing. And every creature which is in heaven, and on the earth, and under the earth, and such as are in the sea, and all that are in them, heard I saying, Blessing, and honour, and glory, and power, be unto him that sitteth upon the throne, and unto the Lamb for ever and ever. And the four beasts said, Amen. And the four and twenty elders fell down and worshipped him that liveth for ever and ever.*
> Revelation 5:11-14

It is interesting to note, that passage lets us know there are animals in Heaven, even before Christ returns.

The *Book of Revelation* goes on to tell us when Christ returns to Earth, He and His followers will come back on white horses.

> *And I saw heaven opened, and behold a white horse; and he that sat upon him was called Faithful and True, and in righteousness he doth judge and make war. His eyes were as a flame of fire, and on his head were many crowns; and he had a name written, that no man knew, but he himself. And he was clothed with a vesture dipped in blood: and his name is called The Word of God. And the armies which were in heaven followed him upon white horses, clothed in fine linen, white and clean.*
> Revelation 19:11-14

That description of Christ's followers riding white horses reminds me of two men who rode white horses. One was

Roy Rogers the other was Jack Wyrtzen.

Roy Rogers was called the *King of the Cowboys*. He was known for riding a Palomino horse named Trigger. I remember seeing Trigger. Trigger appeared golden with a white mane. Technically all Palominos are considered white horses.

The other man, Jack Wyrtzen, was the founder of *Word of Life*. He had a white horse he rode during the rodeo's at the *Word of Life Ranch*.

One time, when he was unable to ride, I had the privilege of riding Jack Wyrtzen's white horse during a rodeo.

Both Roy Rogers and Jack Wyrtzen were born again Christians. They loved animals and the Lord Jesus Christ. That means they will be returning with Jesus and will be riding white horses when they come back with Him. I wonder if they will be riding the same horses they rode while they were here on Earth.

When Jesus returns to Earth, He will set up His millennial rule. That is the thousand year period when He will sit on the throne of David. During that time, He will fulfill all the promises God made to Abraham, Isaac, Jacob, and to all the patriarchs.

During the millennium the world will be different than it is today. There will be no wars. The animal kingdom will also be different.

But with righteousness shall he judge the poor, and reprove with equity for the meek of the earth: and he shall smite the earth with the rod of his mouth, and with the breath of his lips shall he slay the wicked. And righteousness shall be the girdle of his loins, and faithfulness the girdle of his reins. The wolf also shall dwell with the lamb, and the leopard shall lie down with the kid; and the calf and the young lion and the fatling together; and a little child shall lead them. And the cow and the bear shall feed; their young ones shall lie down together: and the lion shall eat straw like the ox. And the sucking child shall play on the hole of the asp, and the weaned child shall put his hand on the cockatrice' den. They shall not hurt nor destroy in all my holy mountain: for the earth shall be full of the knowledge of the LORD, as the waters cover the sea. Isaiah 11:4-9

The Peaceable Kingdom
Painting by Quaker Edward Hicks, 1844-1846

During the millennium there will no longer be any conflict between the animals. They will not harm man or each other. They will all be herbivores again just like before the flood.

During the millennium Satan will be bound. When that time is completed, Satan will lead one final rebellion.

And when the thousand years are expired, Satan shall be loosed out of his prison, And shall go out to deceive the nations which are in the four quarters of the earth, Gog and Magog, to gather them together to battle: the number of whom is as the sand of the sea. And they went up on the breadth of the earth, and compassed the camp of the saints about, and the beloved city: and fire came down from God out of heaven, and devoured them.
Revelation 20:7-9

The amazing thing is many people who lived under Christ's earthy rule during the Millennium, will side with the Devil and oppose Him. That is a very sad truth.

After that final battle is over, this world as we know it will end. There will be the final judgment followed by a new Heaven and a new Earth.

The Last Judgment
Fresco by Michelangelo, Sistine Chapel, 1536-1541

And I saw a great white throne, and him that sat on it, from whose face the earth and the heaven fled away; and there was found no place for them. And I saw the dead, small and great, stand before God; and the books were opened: and another book was opened, which is the book of life: and the dead were judged out of those things which were written in the books, according to their works. And the sea gave up the dead which were in it; and death and hell delivered up the dead which were in them: and they were judged every man according to their works. And death and hell were cast into the lake of fire. This is the second death. And whosoever was not found written in the book of life was cast into the lake of fire. Revelation 20:11-15

Some people say everyone will be in Heaven. In a sense they are correct. Every one will stand before God on that final Judgment Day. The Bible says there will be two groups of people: those whose names are written in the Book of Life; and those who will be judged by their works. The ones whose names are written in the Book of Life are those who one day humbly called upon God to save them. Many people will not do that. They think their works can save them. They will discover they are very wrong.

And I saw a new heaven and a new earth: for the first heaven and the first earth were passed away; and there was no more sea. And I John saw the holy city, new Jerusalem, coming down from God out of heaven, prepared as a bride adorned for her husband. And I heard a great voice out of heaven saying, Behold, the tabernacle of God is with men, and he will dwell with them, and they shall be his people, and God himself shall be with them, and be their God. And God shall wipe away all tears from their eyes; and there shall be no more death, neither sorrow, nor crying, neither shall there be any more pain: for the former things are passed away. And he that sat upon the throne said, Behold, I make all things new. And he said unto me, Write: for these words are true and faithful. And he said unto me, It is done. I am Alpha and Omega, the beginning and the end. I will give unto him that is athirst of the fountain of the water of life freely. Revelation 21:1-6

On that day, sin will finally be destroyed. All things will

be new. That is the day the animals and all creation look forward to. The curse will be over. There will be a joyous celebration for all creation.

Those who one day called upon God and humbly accepted His wonderful gift of salvation will be welcomed into that wonderful place where God lives, along with animals, and all who placed their trust in Him since time began.

Will you be there? If you are not sure, right now you can humbly call upon God to save you from your sin. That will guarantee yourself a place in God's wonderful new kingdom, a place where all men and animals will live together in peace.

Questions for Thought or Discussion
Chapter 11
The End & a New Beginning

1. Is it true one day the world, as we know it, will come to an end? If so, why?

2. What part does man's sin play in bringing our present world to and end?

3. What are the animals waiting for?

4. Which book of the Bible gives us our first glimpse of Heaven?

5. Will there be any animals in Heaven before Christ returns?

6. On what animal will Christ and His followers return to earth?

7. What will be different in the animal kingdom during the millennial rule of Christ on earth?

8. Where will you be when the millennial kingdom ends and there is a new Heaven and new Earth?

Chapter 12

Where Do Animals Go When They Die?

We have now come to the final chapter. It is time to answer the question, *where do animals go when they die?*

Heaven is big enough for all humans and for every animal. However, some teach animals cease to exist when they die and do not go to Heaven. They teach Heaven is only for humans and spiritual beings.

There are numerous problems with that line of reasoning. The other chapters in this book show animals have a body, soul, and spirit, just like man.

We showed how, unlike man, animals do not sin and do not need a Savior.

We saw how animals have a sensitivity to God.

We saw animals have something to say.

We saw God made extraterrestrial beings which have characteristics similar to animals on earth.

We saw there are some animals in Heaven which look just like animals on Earth.

We also saw the animals look forward to the return of Christ. Why would they look forward to the return of Christ is they were not going to spend eternity with Him?

Those facts, all based on clear Biblical teaching, convince me the answer to the question, *where do animas go when they die?* Is simple, they go to Heaven.

There is one passage in Scripture, some use to dispute that conclusion. Let us take a look at that passage.

> *I said in mine heart concerning the estate of the sons of men, that God might manifest them, and that they might see that they themselves are beasts. For that which befalleth the sons of men befalleth beasts; even one thing befalleth them: as the one dieth, so dieth the other; yea,*

they have all one breath; so that a man hath no preeminence above a beast: for all is vanity. All go unto one place; all are of the dust, and all turn to dust again. Who knoweth the spirit of man that goeth upward, and the spirit of the beast that goeth downward to the earth?
Ecclesiastes 3:18-21

Some use this passage to come up with some very faulty opinions. On face value this passage appears to say man and animals are all beasts, and all die and suffer the same fate. The only difference is the spirit of a man goes up and the spirit of beasts go down to the earth.

That passage has been used incorrectly to teach men's spirits go to Heaven and animals do not. If you do not consider the context of this passage, you may come up with that conclusion, but I believe you would be wrong.

It is very important to understand the context of this passage. God had Solomon write the *Book of Ecclesiastes* to show us life apart from God is ultimately meaningless and unfulfilling.

*I the Preacher was king over Israel in Jerusalem. And I gave my heart to seek and search out by wisdom concerning all things that are done **under heaven**: this sore travail hath God given to the sons of man to be exercised therewith. I have seen all the works that are done **under the sun**; and, behold, all is vanity and vexation of spirit.* Ecclesiastes 1:12-14

In Ecclesiastes, Solomon tells how he set out to find meaning and pleasure by pursuing fulfillment from everything possible, apart from God. He reports his activities, his opinions, and his conclusions.

Solomon makes it clear when he is expressing his opinion. He begins such passages with a phrase such as, *I said in my heart*. That makes it clear it is the way he looked at something. Many times he lets us know he discovered his opinions were wrong.

There are two radically different worldviews that affect the way we live and view life. They are contrasted in the Book of Ecclesiastes. The one is called *under the sun* and the other is called *under heaven.*

Under the sun refers to the perspective of someone who lives their life without acknowledging God.

Under heaven refers to the perspective one has when they acknowledge their Creator and seek to follow His principles.

Solomon makes it clear the view that man and animals are both beasts and that the animal's spirits go down to the earth and man's spirits go up in the air, is his own opinion when looking at things *under the sun.*

If you do not look at the context of this passage, and just consider it along with other Old Testament teachings, this verse could be said to teach animals, not man, go to be with God when they die.

The idea of a man's spirit going *up* to be with God is contrary to the Old Testament. Man never went up to be with God until after the resurrection of Christ. In the Old Testament, *the* idea of a spirit going up is more like the wind blowing something worthless away.

Man's Dilemma
Oil Painting by Frans Fracken the Younger, 1633

In the Old Testament when someone died they went

down to the place of the dead. That place was divided into two parts. One part was called *Paradise*, or *Abraham's Bosom*. The righteous, those who sought to honor and follow God, went there. The other part was called *Hell*. The unrighteous dead went there. The unrighteous are those who did not honor or follow God.

> *Hell from beneath is moved for thee to meet thee at thy coming: it stirreth up the dead for thee, even all the chief ones of the earth; it hath raised up from their thrones all the kings of the nations.* Isaiah 14:9

> *Let death seize upon them, and let them go down quick into hell: for wickedness is in their dwellings, and among them.* Psalm 55:15

Jesus validated that concept when He told what happened when a both beggar named Lazarus and a Rich Man died. They both went down to the place of the dead. Lazarus went to *Abraham's Bosom*, the Rich Man to *Hell*.

> *And it came to pass, that the beggar died, and was carried by the angels into Abraham's bosom: the rich man also died, and was buried; And in hell he lift up his eyes, being in torments, and seeth Abraham afar off, and Lazarus in his bosom.* Luke 16:22-23

When Jesus was being crucified, he told one of the thieves who died with Him that the two of them were going to *Paradise*.

> *And Jesus said unto him, Verily I say unto thee, To day shalt thou be with me in paradise.* Luke 23:43

When Christ rose from the dead, He took everyone out of Paradise and *up* to Heaven with Him. Unbelievers remained *down* in Hell. Now, when believers die they go *up* to Heaven not *down* to Paradise.

> *Wherefore he saith, When he ascended up on high, he led captivity captive, and gave gifts unto men.*
> Ephesians 4:8

When the passage in Ecclesiastes is looked out in the

context of the whole book, and in the context of its place in the Old Testament, it does not contradict the conclusion that animals go to Heaven when they die.

Heaven is a beautiful place, it is even more beautiful than the Garden of Eden. One of the most wonderful things about Heaven is there will be no more death, or pain, and there will be no more sin to hurt anyone.

The Garden of Eden
Jan Brueghel the Elder, 1613

It appears the Bible teaches all animals go to Heaven when they die. I find that very encouraging and comforting.

There are a number of animals I look forward to seeing again. I think it is even valid to look forward to having some conversations with them.

It appears clearly to me, the Biblical answer to the question, *where do animals go when they die*, is Heaven.

Now, there is another even more pressing question I must ask you. *Where will you go when you die?*

Unlike the animals, you and I have a sin problem we must deal with, otherwise we will not be going to Heaven. Christ paid the price for your sins and offers you forgiveness and a guarantee of a place in Heaven. All you have to do is realize you are lost and do not deserve Heaven because of your sinfulness. Your only hope of going to Heaven is to recognize you are an unworthy sinner, believe Christ paid the price for your sins, and then humbly call upon Him and accept his forgiveness and receive the gift of salvation. Have you called upon Him and asked Him to save you? If not, why not do that right now?

> *But what saith it? The word is nigh thee, even in thy mouth, and in thy heart: that is, the word of faith, which we preach; That if thou shalt confess with thy mouth the Lord Jesus, and shalt believe in thine heart that God hath raised him from the dead, thou shalt be saved. For with the heart man believeth unto righteousness; and with the mouth confession is made unto salvation. For the scripture saith, Whosoever believeth on him shall not be ashamed. For there is no difference between the Jew and the Greek: for the same Lord over all is rich unto all that call upon him. For whosoever shall call upon the name of the Lord shall be saved.* Romans 10:8-13

A Child Shall Lead Them
Oil Painting by William Strutt, 1896

Questions for Thought or Discussion
Chapter 12
Where Do Animals Go When They Die?

1. Why do animals look forward to the return of Christ?

2. Why did God have Solomon write the Book of Ecclesiastes?

3. What two radically different worldviews are presented in the Book of Ecclesiastes?

4. Where did people go when they died before Christ died on the cross for our sins and then rose from the dead?

5. What happens when people die now?

6. Where do you believe animals go when they die?

7. Where will you go when you die?

Index

Scripture Index
Alphabetical

About the Author

Dr. Larry A. Maxwell is the author of numerous books, including, *More Than 500 Proven Ways to Reduce Expenses, More Than 200 Timeless Truths You Need to Know, Unraveling the Holy Spirit Controversy* and *How to Find the Right Pastor.*

His writing career started when he became the literary editor for his award winning high school yearbook. He later became a journalist and photographer for *The Times of Ti,* the *Glens Falls Post Star* and the *United Press International.* He was honored by The *Associated Press* for his journalism with its First Place Writing Award.

He was a founder and president of *Habitat for Humanity* of Putnam County, New York, and President of the *Hudson Valley Trust.* The Governor of the State of Kentucky honored him for his humanitarian work by conferring on him the title of *Kentucky Colonel.*

He serves as the Town Historian for Patterson, New York, and Director of *The Living History Guild.* He served as the Chairman of *The Company of Military Historians at West Point* and as an advisor for the *History Channel.*

He wrote *Sybil Rides: The True Story of Sybil Ludington the Female Paul Revere, the Burning of Danbury and Battle of Ridgefield.*

He is Pastor of the *Patterson Baptist Church,* the Oldest Baptist Church in New York State and served on the Executive Board of *The Baptist Convention of New York.*

He is a First Responder with the *Patterson Fire Department* where he is the Chaplain, Emergency Medical Technician (EMT) and Fire Police Officer.

You may contact him to order books or to schedule a speaking engagement at his website LarryMaxwell.com.

What Does the Bible Say About Animals?

Larry A. Maxwell

www.ingramcontent.com/pod-product-compliance
Lightning Source LLC
Chambersburg PA
CBHW052115030426
42335CB00025B/3000